All about bodies.

Let's talk about sex.

That's it!

Useful Contacts

FE

af

Y

eters

Contents

"MAN, ARE YOU GAY?"

My heart sank as my friend asked the question I had been avoiding for over four years. What was it about me that gave the gay away? I felt like he had x-ray vision – like he could see past the thin veil hiding my deepest, darkest secret. I hated him for trying to humiliate me in front of a dozen friends, but I knew why he was asking the question. After all, I was the kid who always hung out with girls, wore flared jeans and had no interest in football. At all. What's the point in kicking a ball of air up and down a dirty field? I asked myself, "Should I lie, and protect myself from embarrassment and abuse? Or should I be brave and own my identity with pride, once and for all?" I felt lost and afraid, so I caved and flat-out denied it. "No way. What the hell?" Everyone stayed silent for what felt like a lifetime and then they continued with their mindless chatter, leaving me shaken. I had escaped the nightmare of being found out, just. But from that day on, things changed. People were on to me, and I was becoming less capable of manipulating who I was to survive the warzone that was school, and for that matter, the world. Something had to give or I was going to crumble.

Feeling different. That's where it normally begins for a queer person. You may ask yourself, "Am I broken? Sick? Weird?" The answer is no. There is nothing wrong with you – there's just something slightly different about you. In time, that difference will become the greatest gift you could ask for. It will bring you love, identity, community and eventually the freedom to be yourself. I promise.

Life is a wonderful mess of

successes, mistakes, joy, heartbreak and learning. It can be even more intense if you're gay. In this book, I hope to give you some golden lessons I've learned along the way. Think of me as your supercool gay big brother. Calling myself cool automatically just made me less cool. I am aware of that. Just go with me for a second...

It's been eleven years since I first came out. In that time, I have built a career in television, radio and online, with an audience of almost half a million people, most of whom are LGBT+. Through my work I have received thousands of messages from queer people in every corner of the world. Their experiences have moved and inspired me to fight for us. You will find their stories scattered throughout the pages of this book along with many of my own. Some are shocking, others are utterly embarrassing but most will hopefully inspire you and teach you life skills that I wish I had learned sooner. The names and exact locations of the people who told me their stories have been altered to protect their identities. I'm sound like that.

I've also asked some of the most inspirational gay men I know to tell me what advice they would give to their teenage selves – everyone from Stephen Fry to Shane Jenek (aka Courtney Act). The common theme of their advice is "it gets better". I promise you, they're right – it really does!

I hope this book will become your go-to guide when stuff goes wrong, when stuff goes right or when stuff leaves you confused.

I was once a gay boy, and now I'm a gay man, so this book is mainly focused on the very unique experience of being a cis gay boy (a gay boy whose gender identity matches the sexual characteristics he was born with). There are of course many aspects of this book that will resonate with lesbians, bi girls, trans people, non-binary people, intersex people, asexual people and anyone else from our gorgeous queer community. Everyone in our community experiences a different journey, so it would be unfair for me to try and tell everyone's stories.

I hope this book will become your go-to guide when stuff goes wrong, when stuff goes right or when stuff leaves you confused. You can read it cover to cover or pick out certain sections but most of all, have fun with it. Rip out pages, scribble on it, take pictures of bits and most importantly, share it. This book is designed for everyone and that includes friends, families, teachers and even bullies. Even if you're not a gay boy, I believe the stories within these pages will help you support, understand and love your gay brother/friend/cousin/classmate in the way he needs it most. That's why I've asked my parents to write a section specifically for your family to read. Their journey to understanding and supporting you is just as important as yours, so please hand this to them too.

I've gone from being a lonely, lost and afraid 13-year-old boy to a confident, caring, content and proud gay 27-year-old man. I dedicate this book to you and the millions of beautiful gay boys around the world fighting to find themselves and the love they deserve.

So you think you might be gay...

WHY DO I FEEL DIFFERENT?

Why do I feel all fuzzy and weird when I look at that guy? Why don't I feel the same way when I look at girls?

This question has gone through millions of gay boys' heads since, well, forever! The fuzzy feeling can pop up like an unexpected boner (more on those to come) and can go away just as fast. Just remember that it's okay, it's normal and it's not something you need to change.

Let's call that feeling a "tingle". I had my first tingle for a guy when I was about seven years old, watching the Disney movie *Aladdin*. Yes, my first crush was on a cartoon character. At least he was human! Princess Jasmine, his love interest, was just an annoying bystander to me. I was incredibly envious of her because she got to hug and kiss my Arabian prince. Aladdin had gorgeous olive skin, wavy black hair and a cheeky boy-next-door smile. I was mesmerised. I didn't know it then, but, a baby gay was born that day.

> **It's okay, it's normal and it's not something you need to change.**

Figuring out if you're gay isn't a complicated scientific process – it simply comes down to how you feel. Only YOU can know what's going on inside your head. Being attracted to someone of the same sex doesn't necessarily mean you're gay or bi. Maybe you just admire their talents or their personality. Even though I'm super gay, I was obsessed with one of my first teachers, Miss Donovan. Her hair was always perfect, she was so friendly and she smelled of what I now know is Burberry Weekend perfume. (Sometimes I shock myself with how wonderfully gay I am. What other male student would have been able to pinpoint a perfume brand at the age of ten? Being gay really is a superpower.) I thought I had a crush on Miss Donovan, but it turned out I just idolized her – I didn't have romantic feelings for her.

So try not to jump to any conclusions about your sexuality. Allow yourself time to feel different things and don't shut any of them out. If you find your eyes wandering and looking at other boys, then let them. If they wander and look at girls too, that's cool. Allow yourself to fantasise about being close to the person who has caught your eye and see how it feels. Eventually you'll know what feels natural for you. Maybe you're attracted to men, or women, or men and women, or non-binary people. Or maybe you don't have sexual feelings for anyone. However you feel, it's valid.

If you've realized you're probably not straight, then you've reached what I like to call the PCO or Pre-Coming-Out stage. This is one of the most important stages of your journey – the moment you have to say the words you may have been afraid of to yourself: "I am gay". (Or queer, or bi...) My PCO took about four years. I tried to trick myself into being straight by thinking about boobs non-stop and ignoring guys who were totally stunning and, in hindsight, deserved my undivided gay attention. There's one thing I now know for sure: no matter how hard you try and fight it, YOU CANNOT CHANGE WHO YOU ARE. The longer you try to suppress the real you, the longer and harder your PCO will be.

One thing that holds many people back is the fear that once they come out, they'll have to start acting like the stereotypes of gay characters you see on TV. I am here to tell you that's not the case (unless that's who you naturally are, in which case shine baby, shine!). Coming out to yourself frees you to be more yourself than you've ever been before. LGBT+ people come in all shapes, sizes and colours. They have infinite interests, talents, personalities and flaws. Just flick through this book and see what other gay men have achieved. These men and millions like them are proof that our big gay family can do and be anything!

PCO
"Pre-Coming-Out Stage"

noun • The period of a queer person's life between their first realization that they're not straight, and when they come out to their friends and family.

Jorge from Mexico remembers his first gay feelings:

"I always knew my sexuality was different from my friends'. I heard how they spoke about girls, saying things like, "She's so cute!". I never felt that way. As the years went by, my confusion just spiralled. I felt like I didn't fit in. But when I was 11, I had my first wet dream and everything clicked. I dreamed I was in a relationship with Lionel Messi, the footballer. I'm not even a football fan! I woke up the next morning, feeling like I finally understood myself. I felt so relieved in the dream, so free and so at home. It felt like finding a pair of shoes that fit perfectly."

Stephen Fry

Stephen Fry is a writer, actor, comedian, presenter and activist. He's written novels, non-fiction books, screenplays, musicals and comedy sketches. With Hugh Laurie, he's half of the comedy double act Fry and Laurie. And he's the voice of the Harry Potter audio books!

Stephen, it's going to be fine. The world will change for the better. It will be achingly slow but the light will break through the clouds, I promise. Live an honest open life and people won't despise you for it, or if they do they won't be worth knowing: only insecure and unhappy people snigger and sneer. One day – you won't believe this now – but one day you'll even be able to marry another man, and it will seem the easiest and most natural thing in the world. The only story will be that there is no story. Just wait, the tide will turn.

2

LGBTTQQIAAP+

What does that mess of letters and symbols mean?!

I'm going to use the acronym LGBT+ (which stands for lesbian, gay, bisexual, trans, plus) in this book to stand for our big diverse queer community. This is a shortening of a much longer acronym that also includes queer, questioning, intersex, asexual, ally, pansexual... and this STILL leaves some people out! Figuring out who you are and where you fit on the ever-growing rainbow of identities is a bit like looking for the perfect pairs of jeans. You'll know when you find something fits, because it will feel like a second skin. In other words, the questioning stage – the time you take to figure out your identity – is worth it. You might not feel like any of the labels is right for you. That's fine too. Labels can be limiting and come with a bunch of stereotypes, but they can also help you feel less lost or lonely. They can help you find a community of like-minded people – people who will probably become your best friends and supporters, because they know what it's like to be gay/lesbian/bi/pansexual/queer/trans. Being heard and understood will empower you and help build your self-confidence. But remember that your character, interests, style and soul shouldn't change to "match" your newfound identity. Your identity just reflects the beautiful person you already are.

Also, it's totally possible to have feelings for – or even have sex with – people who are the same gender as you and not to identify as gay, or bi. And it's possible to identify as gay and still get the odd crush on girls. You do you!

There are hundreds of recognized gender identities and sexual orientations with more being discovered every day. Listing all of them here would likely take up more than half of this book so let's just focus on the most common ones.

BI
A term used to describe attraction towards more than one gender.

CISGENDER
Someone whose gender identity is the same as the sex they were assigned at birth.

GAY
Refers to a man who's attracted to men, or a woman who's attracted to women.

ACE
A term used to describe a variation in levels of romantic/sexual attraction, including a lack of attraction. Ace people may describe themselves as asexual, aromantic, demis and grey-As.

ALLY
Someone (usually straight and/or cis) who supports members of the LGBT+ community.

INTERSEX
A term used to describe a person who may have the biological attributes of both sexes or whose biological attributes do not fit with societal assumptions about what constitutes male or female. Intersex people may identify as male, female or non-binary.

LESBIAN

Refers to a woman who's attracted to women.

NON-BINARY

An umbrella term for people whose gender identity doesn't sit comfortably with "man" or "woman". Some non-binary people identify with some aspects of binary identities, while others reject them entirely. Sometimes shortened to NB or enby.

PAN

Refers to a person whose attraction towards others isn't limited by sex or gender.

QUEER

In the past, this was a derogatory term for LGBT+ people, but the term has now been reclaimed by LGBT+ people – particularly young people – who don't identify with the traditional categories of gender identity and sexual orientation. Some LGBT+ people still regard it as a derogatory term.

QUESTIONING

The process of exploring your sexuality or gender identity.

TRANS

An umbrella term to describe people whose gender is not the same as, or does not sit comfortably with, the sex they were assigned at birth.

3

FIRST CRUSH

Boys, boys, boys.

They will be the source of endless learning, heartbreak, lust and love throughout your life. Some will come and go so fast you'll be left with love whiplash. Others will stick around for longer and make a lifelong impression on you. Boys can be terrible (I'm not bitter, promise). But they can also be incredible one-person joy factories that will bring you endless passion and love. No matter how many guys become part of your journey, there's nothing quite like the tsunami of emotions that comes with your first gay crush.

The first time most of us fall in love, it's with a straight boy who's oblivious to our affections. Your first crush probably won't turn out to be your Prince Charming, but you'll still learn a lot from falling for him. My first crush was the unforgettable Sam. He taught me how to deal with unrequited love and rejection – skills that came in VERY handy a decade later when I found myself in the war zone of online dating – and he truly helped me accept my gayness. I never got to thank him for that, sadly. He was a work of art – he looked as though he had just stepped out of a high-school movie with his chiselled facial features, cheeky grin, boyish confidence and smooth, tanned skin … and he had a body that would make you go weak at the knees. He was one of the rugby guys, and I knew he was pretty much off limits for me. But that didn't stop me strategically choosing my classroom seat so that I could spend the 45-minute period staring longingly across the room at him, wondering, "What if?"

That might make me sound like a bit of a creep, but I was obsessed with him. In a time before internet porn, just looking at him was enough to get me going. Simpler times...

I never had the confidence to declare my love to Sam, but some boys do tell their crushes how they feel. Calum from London was one of those boys:

"There was something extraordinarily ordinary about my first crush. He wasn't particularly good looking and he told terrible jokes. He always smelled like cheap deodorant and Brylcreem, but I found it absolutely intoxicating. He broke my heart every time his eyes lit up as a beautiful girl walked in the room, but I never gave up hoping that there was something more to our friendship. Our Friday night sleepovers were the highlight of my week, and I felt a dizzying happiness in staying up all night with him, watching cheesy movies and eating snacks stolen from our parents' kitchens. He was my whole world, and I couldn't imagine a future without him. I was 15 when I told him I'd been harbouring feelings for him for almost two years. He didn't take it well. He slammed the door so hard on his way out that it shattered one of the hinges, and I never saw him again. It took me a long time to get over that. But on my 16th birthday, a card fell through the door. It was from him. He said how sorry he was, and that he hoped I'd find someone special. Almost 12 years later, I'm still looking, but I'll never forget the way he made me feel. I see a little bit of him in every guy I've ever dated, and after all this time the smell of Brylcreem still takes me back and makes me wonder what he's doing now."

4

GENDER IDENTITY

I was king of the sissy boys growing up.

I loved running around the house in my mother's pink silk night-gown, black stilettos and anything I could find that sparkled. I hadn't yet been affected by the suffocating expectations of masculinity that society imposes on us boys. My fun was swiftly ended by my father, who ordered me to start acting like a boy. The only problem was that, for me, this was what boyhood was all about. I thought, "I like being a boy. I also like dresses and pretty things. I want to be a boy who can sometimes wear dresses and pretty things." To seven-year-old Riyadh, it was that simple. To everyone else, it broke some invisible law of boyhood and I had to be stopped before I embarrassed myself and my family. I remember feeling lost for a while. I knew I liked "girly" things, but I knew I couldn't have them. Why? Because I was a boy. It seemed like the biggest injustice in the world. I began to think, "If I want to be happy, then I'll probably have to be a girl." But I was wrong.

Sex is about your anatomy – you're assigned "male" or "female'" at birth depending on whether you're born with a penis or a vagina. But **gender** is different. It's about how society expects you to behave as a result of your sex. You know the stereotypes – girls are supposed to like pink things, and crying at rom coms. Boys are supposed to be strong and not show their emotions, and like sports and cars. But who says pink is for girls? As late as 1927, *Time* magazine was recommending that boys be dressed in pink and girls in blue! And who says that boys can't wear make-up? Until the mid-19th century, both men and women wore it.

Your **gender identity** is different again – it's your understanding of yourself as male or female, or a mixture of both, or neither, and how you present yourself to the world. It goes far beyond liking pink and sequins, or fighting and cars. Your gender identity can be the same as the sex you were assigned at birth, or different. Transgender people have a gender identity that's different from the sex they were assigned at birth. Some trans people go through a "transition'" to try to align their internal gender with their outward appearance. Some start wearing clothes that are associated with the opposite gender and change the pronouns they use – from "he/ him" to "she/ her", for example. Some change their bodies by taking drugs or having surgery.

The gender binary – the idea that there are just two genders: male and female – is pretty

> **The gender binary – the idea that there are just two genders: male and female – is pretty old-fashioned. Gender is a spectrum.**

BOTH

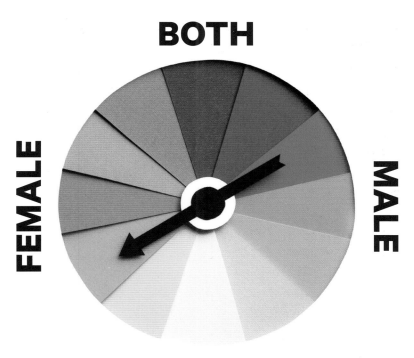

FEMALE

MALE

NEITHER

old-fashioned. Gender is a spectrum. Some people whose gender identity doesn't fit within the traditional categories of male or female classify themselves as non-binary, or genderqueer, and lots of them prefer gender-neutral pronouns, like "they/them", "xe" or "hir".

Gender identity and sexual orientation are two completely separate things. Trans and non-binary people can be gay, straight, bi or pansexual – who you're attracted to has nothing to do with your gender identity. If gender is a sliding scale from female to male, I would say that I'm comfortable with my male identity as long as I can occasionally wander into that glorious middle ground. It's only now, aged 27, that I have managed to shake off some of the gender shackles placed on me as a kid. I now mix pieces from the women's section into my wardrobe and allow the femme inside me to shine after years of trying to suppress her. It's fun not caring what people think!

Being proud of your identity is a massive part of the journey to self-love. Many trans people start out thinking that in order to be happy they'll have to "pass" as cisgender. The truth is, being trans is beautiful. But a 2017 survey conducted by LGBT+ rights charity Stonewall showed that almost half of trans students in the UK had attempted suicide. It's a shocking statistic that proves just how difficult it is for young people who struggle with their gender identity. It's important to know that if you are going through a tough time, there is help out there. Check out the Useful Contacts section at the back of this book for helpful numbers and websites. You have a family of people cheering you on all over the world.

> **Many trans people start out thinking that in order to be happy they'll have to "pass" as cisgender. The truth is, being trans is beautiful.**

The battle for acceptance currently faced by the trans community in the UK and US is similar to the one fought by gay men and lesbians 20 years ago. It's SO important for the queer community to stand shoulder to shoulder at all times. We are so much stronger together.

I asked my friend Paris Lees, a trans activist, writer and broadcaster, what she would say to her 16-year-old self about her gender identity:

"I know you desperately want to go off and blend in as a girl, but one day you'll feel proud of who you are. Believe it or not, being trans is going to become cool. Trans women will star in TV shows and win awards and appear on the cover of Vogue."

Jamie, a non-binary person from Stockholm, wrote to me about the journey to what they call "home":

"When I was twelve, I was so confused. I tried to become more like a 'dude', but I was pretending to be someone that I wasn't, and it was so tiring. I tried everything – I had long hair and short hair, I wore dresses, I wore suits, I dated a guy, I dated a girl. Nothing felt like 'home'. But now I realize that I am both genders and neither. I think we're all just souls that ride in human bodies. Souls and energy have no gender and neither do I :)"

5

ANXIETY & WORRY

"Relax. You're fine, I'm fine, everything is going to be fine. Worrying that something awful is about to happen doesn't mean that thing is any more or less likely to happen. Let go of those thoughts and just live."
—Lorraine Khalaf (my mom)

Anxiety is the worst. As humans, there's no escaping this weird, fear-inducing, shaky feeling that washes over us when we least expect it. Unlike a physical injury, people cannot always see that you're suffering from anxiety. Even if they do know, they may not understand enough about how anxiety works to be able to help you. This makes the whole thing even more difficult. When you're feeling anxious, you may be physically present in a room but only 30% there mentally, because of the sea of thoughts rushing through your brain.

My battle with chronic anxiety began when I was nine years old. A few things happened to trigger it: my grandfather died, and my little brother had a couple of scary episodes where he stopped breathing. I started having major panic attacks whenever my mother left the house without me. I truly believed that when she walked out of the door, I'd never see her again. I had visions of her suffering a bad road traffic accident or being stabbed in a car park. She would go out for Chinese food with her friends and I would call her every half an hour to make sure she was still alive.

At the time, counselling and therapy weren't the norm, so I struggled for a long time by myself. My mother eventually sat me down and talked to me – she reassured me that worrying about something didn't mean it was more likely to happen, and that everything was going to be fine.

After that, I began to take control of my feelings, but I lived with low-level anxiety for years, until I was about 23. Then, after another death in my family and the end of a long-term relationship, the panic came rushing back, hard. This time I went for Cognitive Behavioural Therapy and it saved me. I have laid out some of the tools I learned in my therapy sessions in this chapter. I use them every day to feel calm, centred and at peace, and to accept what I cannot control. Try them if you're feeling anxious or depressed, and tell a parent, teacher or doctor what you're going through. There is no shame in asking for help and you won't regret it.

Anxiety is like a creepy friend who sneaks up behind you and whispers random worries into your ear. Worries you never knew you had. They silently lurk there and follow you around day to day. Nobody else can see or hear them. The more you try to make sense of the worries, the more overwhelming and confusing they can become. If your anxiety gets really bad, your thoughts begin to spiral and you might lose the ability to do everyday things like going to school, listening to people, having a conversation, laughing or eating properly.

THE UPSIDE TO ANXIETY

It's hard to believe when you're in the middle of a panic attack, but anxiety can actually be useful. Imagine you're a Stone Age guy, about to attacked by a woolly mammoth. You need to get out of that situation, and fast. Your body releases a hormone called adrenaline that makes your body react more quickly. Your heart rate speeds up, pumping more blood to your muscles, getting them ready for action. Your breathing becomes more rapid, bringing more oxygen to the brain. Your pupils dilate, allowing more light to hit your retinas and make you more alert. This is great of you're about to run a marathon, perform at a pop concert or escape a pack of lions, but for most of us, this isn't what we get up to on a given Wednesday afternoon.

It's totally normal to feel anxious before an interview, a school play or a first date. That's part of the excitement of life. But the world we live in contains endless triggers that can set off anxiety. Maybe you didn't finish your school assignment or your new Insta selfie only got two likes, or your crush is walking towards you and you don't know what to say... If you start feeling anxious all the time, or if you have panic attacks, then take action to pull yourself back to the safety zone.

Tips to help get your anxiety under control

RECOGNIZE IT

Some people suggest shrugging off worry or anxiety and powering on with your day. DO NOT DO THIS. Even if you can ignore the thoughts and feelings, which is difficult, they will lie dormant and might become a bigger problem down the line. Get to know your mind and body. When you feel anxious, say to yourself, "Okay. I feel anxious." And try to accept it. Ground yourself. Feel your feet on the ground. Sit down, or stand against a wall. Begin breathing slowly in through your nose for three seconds and out through your mouth for three seconds. Try to count your breaths and come back to the present moment.

QUESTION IT

Work out if there was a particular thought that led to the anxiety or panic attack. Then try challenging the thought. Maybe you jumped to the worst-case scenario – just because you haven't finished your homework, that doesn't mean you'll be suspended. If people haven't liked your Insta selfie, that doesn't mean they don't like you. They might be busy doing other things. See if you can replace your negative thoughts with positive ones. This panic and this situation will not kill you.

BE MINDFUL. THROW AWAY THE FEELING

This is the most important aspect of taking back control – it's a concept that saved me from countless panic attacks and gave me my life back when I was feeling broken and spiralling.

Practise being in the present moment – not the present day, or hour, or minute, but this very second. Ask yourself: What can I see? What can I taste? What can I hear? What can I touch? Concentrating on the things around you will get you out of your head and back in the present moment. Anxiety is worry about the future – and the future doesn't exist. Things that happened yesterday are gone and can't be changed, let them go. Be in the moment, this moment, right now. It's the only thing that's real, and the only thing you can control.

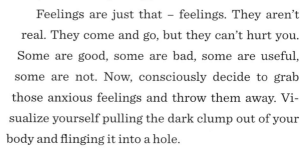

Feelings are just that – feelings. They aren't real. They come and go, but they can't hurt you. Some are good, some are bad, some are useful, some are not. Now, consciously decide to grab those anxious feelings and throw them away. Visualize yourself pulling the dark clump out of your body and flinging it into a hole.

Other ways to break the anxiety cycle

- Chat to family and friends about it – a problem shared is a problem halved

- Treat yourself to your fave guilty pleasure movie (*Titanic* for me, every time)

- Exercise. This releases natural happy hormones called endorphins

- Go for a walk to clear your head

- Make a list of the tasks that are making you stressed and work through them one by one. Ticking them off one by one feels incredible

- Learn a new skill. Putting time and energy into a fresh passion can give you a sense of purpose and direction

- Cut out caffeinated drinks – they can give you palpitations and trigger anxiety

- Reduce your time online. It's not the real world and playing catch up with likes and followers will make you feel inadequate. You are enough as you are

- Get eight hours sleep every night. Your brain needs time to rest, recharge and flush out chemicals after a long day

- If someone is bugging you or getting you down, politely ask to speak to them privately. See if you can resolve the situation – getting that off your chest will free you to focus on what's important. They may even thank you for it!

Try a mixture of these tricks – but if you find yourself feeling down or anxious a lot of the time, ask for help. Turn to the back of the book for a list of organizations that might be able to help you.

If you're feeling anxious right now, breathe in for a count of three, then breathe out for a count of three. And remember you're not alone. I wrote this chapter while I was suffering from an anxiety attack.

6

THE GIFT OF GAYNESS

I never thought I'd reach a point where I'd see my gayness as a "gift", but I've been out for decade now, and I can honestly say that I wouldn't change who I am for the world.

Being gay has brought me endless happiness, exciting opportunities, freedom, friends and a chosen family of people all over the world. It's like a license to be whoever and whatever I want to be and it has helped me realize that not caring about other people's opinions is a great strength.

The journey towards accepting your sexuality as a gift instead of something to be ashamed of isn't always a quick or easy one. It can take many years of living an open and authentic life and allowing yourself to

The journey towards accepting your sexuality as a gift instead of something to be ashamed of isn't always a quick or easy one.

learn from many glorious mistakes along the way. Eventually you get to send the elevator of self-acceptance down to the next wave of baby gays. That's sort of what I'm doing right now... *DING!* Hop on in!

Here are just some of the things I love about being gay:

You never take your freedom – or your love – for granted

I still feel a special and unique kind of luck every single time I kiss my boyfriend. It's a feeling I'm not sure straight people ever experience. I feel lucky that I can experience love and express my sexuality without worrying that someone will tell me that what I'm doing is wrong. I don't take my freedom for granted, because it was illegal for two men to have sex in Ireland until 1993 and in fourteen states in the USA it was banned until 2003! Sure, some would say it's sad that I should feel lucky to kiss someone I love, but I choose to see the positive in it, to savour every magical second of intimacy with another man, on my terms, without fear.

You're automatically part of a community of amazing people

When you come out, there isn't a secret initiation ceremony where you are anointed with the sacred tears of RuPaul while musical theatre classics play in the background. Although that would be AMAZING. But you do get to find your new chosen family – the community of hundreds of millions of LGBT+ people around the world who have your back and understand who you are, even if you've never met them.

It tunes you into injustice

Being gay forces you to look inward and ask, "What really matters? Why am I here and what can I add to a world that has, at times, let me down?" Life can be hard for queer people but we can learn so much and grow stronger through our struggles. Because you've suffered injustice, it's easier for you to spot it, and you're more likely to stand up for the rights of other people.

You get to be yourself

It's horrible to feel like you're faking it to get by. I'm so much happier now that I accept who I really am. Being an openly gay man means I get to own my true identity and celebrate myself for exactly who I am. And it means I care less about what people think of me, too.

Declan from Ireland describes why he's grateful to be gay:

"Gay men appreciate some things more because we have to seek them out – the world isn't set up to automatically provide us with friendships, relationships, marriage and a family. And honestly, it feels like we're the select few kids born with magic – like we were chosen to go to Hogwarts. We have our battles to fight, but we get to spread our magic to the outside world, and when the world lets itself, it values what we have to offer."

Clark Moore

Clark Moore has been acting since he was seven years old. His big break came when he won the part of Ethan in the movie *Love, Simon*.

Relax! Take a deep breath. The things that feel very big right now won't matter very soon. Your relationship with your identity will evolve faster if you stop associating your identity with your worth. Trust your instincts, don't allow yourself to be made to believe things that you know to be untrue, and don't take anything personally.

Coming out.

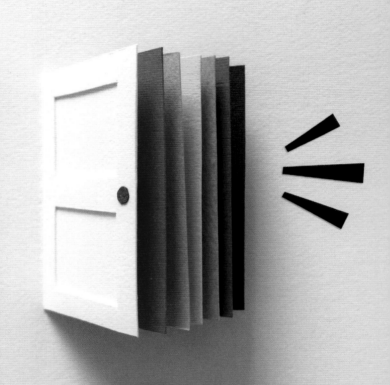

7

I'M COMING OUT

In an ideal world, LGBT+ people wouldn't need to come out.

Society would accept that everyone is different and that there is no such thing as "normal", and your sexuality would be as interesting as your eye colour (i.e. not very). Unfortunately, we don't live in that kind of world (yet), so people assume you're straight or cisgender unless you tell them otherwise. And they expect you declare who you fancy, even though it's nobody's business. Humans are weird.

If you're reading this, you probably know and accept that you're not straight. CONGRATULATIONS! This is a massive step and I want you to know that I am here with party poppers, celebrating that achievement for you, because coming out to *yourself* is the biggest challenge and now that part is behind you. You inspire me!

First things first – YOU DON'T NEED TO COME OUT RIGHT NOW. You can do it whenever and however you want. Tell one person, tell loads of people, tell your dog, organize a flashmob, write a letter, draw it in the sand, send a text message, write a song. There are countless ways

You can come out whenever and however you want.

to do it and none of them are wrong. This is your story to tell and you can take as much time as you want with it.

I wish I could give you a step-by-step guide to coming out, but I can't, because everyone's situation is different. For some people, coming out is dangerous: there are many countries around the world where being gay is still illegal, and many religions teach that being gay is a sin. But if you're reading this, you probably live in a place where it's okay to be gay. You might think your family will react really badly, or maybe you don't think they'll mind at all. But even if your parents go on pride marches and watch *Priscilla, Queen of the Desert* on repeat, coming out is still one of the scariest things you'll ever do. Coming out takes courage, but one thing is for sure: it'll change your life for the better, forever.

The likelihood is that you WILL NOT need to worry about the

THINGS to CONSIDER
before you make that jump into a life of openness and freedom.

Have I heard my family members express homophobic views, or do I have any LGBT+ relatives who experienced a bad reaction when they came out?

If so, you might want to wait until you know you can support your-self independently before you come out to them. That doesn't mean you have to keep your sexuality a secret from everyone, though – you can still tell your friends, as long as you know it won't get back to your family. If you don't know what your parents think about LGBT+ peo-ple, try telling them about a fake person at school or university who has just come out, and see what they say.

things to consider I've listed below. Your family might weep a little, hug you a lot, and throw you a big gay party. But having an understanding of your situation and how you can react to different outcomes will allow you to breathe a little easier during this transformative process.

Alex from The Netherlands told me about the joy of being out to his friends:

"During the week, I'm at university, so I can do whatever I want and basically be myself. But at the weekend, when I come back home, I have to behave like another person, that person I was pretending to be all those years when I was growing up. I really, really, really feel better now that I can be a hundred percent myself with my friends."

Do I have somewhere to stay in case I need time away from my immediate family?

It's very unlikely you'll need to, but it's a good idea to check you if can stay with a friend or a family member just in case.

Is there an LGBT+ youth centre near me?

It's great to have a support network ready just in case. There are organizations that can provide emergency help and advice if you need it.

 Turn to the Useful Contacts section at the back of this book for a list of useful organizations.

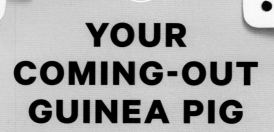

8

YOUR COMING-OUT GUINEA PIG

Before you come out, think about the first person you should tell.

Think of them as your own personal coming-out guinea pig. It could be one of your closest friends, your favourite aunt, that teacher who just gets you, or anyone else who you feel happy and safe around. They should be someone you can trust to keep the news to themselves – someone who's likely to support you on this wonderful journey.

I didn't make it easy for myself – I decided to tell my closest three girlfriends AT THE SAME TIME! I told them all to meet me during our school lunchbreak for "some news". I was always so bloody dramatic. I was trembling from head to toe because I had never said the words aloud before. At that time, I believed I was bisexual – I was afraid of committing to being 100% gay in case I wanted to be with a girl one day. I thank heteronormative social conditioning for that!

The girls and I walked around the school building over and over until I finally plucked up the courage to look at them in the eye and say, "I'm bi." They didn't even blink. One gave me a hug, and the others said they were totally fine about it. We talked about how long I had known, and the school day went on as though I had just told them I was going to get highlights in my hair at the weekend. (I told them that too, in fairness.) I didn't get the massive fireworks or screaming biphobia I had expected. In a way, I was disappointed by how much of a non-event it was!

Although I trusted and loved these girls – I still do – before I knew it, my secret had spread through the 800 students at my school like homosexual wildfire. Everyone seemed to know within a matter of days. It felt IDENTICAL to that scene in

Telling a group in the early stages can leave you open to gossip – everyone loves to talk, and there's no gossip quite like someone coming out at school.

Love, Simon when Simon walks into school the day after he is outed online. I felt like everyone was looking at me and talking about me, and that things were moving in slow motion. I was upset that I didn't get to tell everyone myself, but I was also relieved that I didn't have to.

I'm not telling you this to freak you out, but to encourage you to tell one person at a time. Telling a group in the early stages can leave you open to gossip – everyone loves to talk, and there's no gossip quite like someone coming out at school. People need a hobby, I swear.

Trevor from Boston told me about the amazing friend he had by his side when he was coming out:

"I knew I needed help, but I was too afraid and ashamed to talk to anyone. But one day, my best friend came to me and said, 'Are you ok? Because I know there's something wrong. Please, just tell me.' I told her everything, and I was so relieved. It's amazing how powerful simple words can be. Talking to someone is probably one of the most effective medicines. And I think everyone has the right to be listened to. Since then, my life has completely changed, and I'm so grateful to that girl. She was the only one who tried to help me, and still helps me now, whenever I feel low or when I'm paralyzed by anxiety.

Coming out is hard – it's a journey into the unknown. But remember, even though you may not be able to see us just yet, you have a family of hundreds of millions of people around the world who are silently cheering you on.

We are here for you.

We are waiting for you!

9

MY COMING-OUT STORY

Writing this book has been a difficult but hugely rewarding process for me.

I want to give you the most unfiltered and honest advice I can, but to do that I've had to drag myself back to some of the most upsetting moments of my life – moments that almost broke me, but that helped me grow into the person I am today. Nothing encapsulates that combination of pain and triumph more than my coming out story. It shows how things can go from worst-case scenario to best-case scenario with time, love and understanding.

After four years of keeping my sexuality to myself, the secret was consuming me. It felt like a pot of water that was bubbling violently, higher and higher. I was terrified of coming out, but I felt I was losing control, and that the words "I'M GAY!" were ready to come flying out at any random person. Why now? Why me? I wanted it to go away. Plus I was a young red-blooded male, so I was a thundering ball of frustrated libido. Something as vanilla as a topless guy in a TV advert would leave me with a beating heart, wide eyes and a semi in my pants. Not ideal when you're watching *Coronation Street* with your parents!

I started watching porn on the family computer whenever the house was empty. One day I made the error of leaving the browser window open on one of the sites ... You can imagine what happened next, right?

I left the house and my mom went to use the computer. To her shock she was greeted with page after page of soft-core gay porn. To her it was obvious who had been looking at this stuff – she ruled my outrageously heterosexual father and little brother out.

Later that night she came to me as I sat alone in the kitchen and said, "Riyadh, is there something you'd like to tell me? You know you can say anything to me." My mind began to race – I was trying to think of something she might be alluding to, apart from my sexuality. ANYTHING. But I couldn't. My heart sank and I put my head in my hands. I was filled with a suffocating wave of fear, shame and embarrassment. My cover was blown, but I still didn't fully love myself, so it was almost impossible for me to say "Yes. I'm gay."

Mom kept trying to get my attention but I was afraid to let her look into my eyes – eyes that she had been able to read like a book since the day I was born. After three hours of crying, I eventually turned my puffy, tear-covered face towards her. She looked into my eyes and instantly knew her hunch was correct. At the time, I told her that I was bisexual. As I've said, I thought there was a chance I might want to be with a woman one day. I was wrong.

Over the following months, I felt lighter, happier and more "me" than I had for years. I soon found myself exclusively attracted to guys. Sorry ladies. I just flowed with my feelings and didn't resist. Mom and I would look at guys walking down the street as we drove in the car together. She would occasionally gesture to a hottie and ask, "Would you?" And I would reply "ABSOLUTELY!". We grew closer than ever before. She knew I had been through years of silent struggles and pain, so now she was doing everything she could to normalize my feelings, to validate me and to help me feel safe. There was one problem though...

We both knew the news of my homosexuality was likely to hit my dad hard. He was an Iraqi-born man's man who owned a mechanics garage and loved watching football and boxing. I mean, you get the picture, right? Coming out to him was a terrifying prospect. I already felt I had let him down time after time by not wanting to learn karate, by dressing in my mother's clothes, by having limp wrists and an effeminate voice. Was this news going to push him over the edge?

In the nine months after I came out to Mom, I drifted further and further away from Dad. I now realize I was subconsciously detaching myself from him – I had predicted what his reaction to my news would be and I was trying to protect myself. I would leave the room when he walked in, I'd only speak to him when I had to, and I would disregard and contradict anything he said. To Dad I was just a moody teenager, but in reality I was punishing him in advance for the way I knew he was going to make me feel when he learned who I really was.

SUPER DRAMATIC THINGS

I thought would happen when Dad found out:

- I'd be kicked out of the house and become homeless
- I'd be "honour killed" in my sleep
- I'd be forced into an arranged marriage with a woman
- I'd be sent for gay conversion therapy
- I'd be abandoned by my father forever
- I'd be physically beaten by my father or someone else.

One night, after an argument with my dad, I grabbed my jacket, swore at my parents and ran into the night, alone. I wanted to get away from that house, from him and from my own fears and shame. But I also wanted Dad to need me. He chased after me that night, and I felt a strange sort of comfort. He still loved me and wanted me as his son, if though I knew that might change when he found out I was gay. Growing up gay in a straight boy's world can make you CRAZY.

And then one day, over dinner, my mom said: "Riyadh, I think it's time for you to tell your dad something." Had I heard her correctly?? I started to panic, and said, "Shut up, Mom! Shut up!" But Mom kept pushing, and I realized it was now or never.

I tried to form the words to tell Dad the truth, but my mouth wouldn't open. So I picked up a school book that was lying on the table, tore out the back page and wrote the words "I'm gay". Through tears, I slid the page over to my dad.

There was a pause that seemed to last a lifetime. And then he gave me a loose huge and said, in an unsure voice, "Everything will be okay". After that, he locked himself in the bathroom for an hour.

The following days were tough. Dad seemed like a zombie. He would float in and out of the house expressionless, without saying a word to any of us. He'd always had this knowing, caring, magical glint in his eye when he looked at me. It's hard to describe, but it was full of love and pride. Now, that glint was gone.

After a week or so, my mom started to worry about him. She asked me to talk to him. Reluctantly, I took a beer out to him in the garden and asked if he was okay. He didn't answer. I lost my temper. I told him I was normal and that I was still his son. I said I had always been gay and that I would love to bring a boyfriend home to meet him one day. That's when things really went downhill.

Dad dropped to his knees and began to cry. "Why you?" he said. "Why do you have to be gay? It's not right!" I couldn't believe what I was seeing – the man I loved most in the world, the man who had taught me what was right and wrong, the man I saw as my beacon of strength was on the ground at my feet, broken and weeping. What made it worse was that *I* had broken him and I didn't know how to make it better. I wasn't going to change, because I knew I couldn't change.

But over the following months, things began to get better. I gave Dad space to breathe, to get used to having a gay son and to realize that I was the EXACT same person that I had been before. He spoke to other fathers of gay sons about their experiences and how they coped. He listened to my mother when she pointed out that he cared about his family more than anything in the world. He began to communicate with me again. We laughed at the TV together, he made light-hearted jokes again, and the father I knew and loved came back into my life. After about a year, the loving glint returned to his eyes when he looked at me. He started to hug and kiss me again. He even became interested in LGBT+ equality. WHAT? YES!

It's been a decade since the night Dad fell to his knees. He's now an activist who fights for the rights of LGBT+ people alongside me and my mom. He has been to gay music festivals, he's friends with drag queens, he has marched in countless pride events, he has spoken about his experience as a father of a gay man on TV and radio shows, he campaigned for same-sex marriage in Ireland and held my hand as we watched the results of the vote being read out, he has welcomed my boyfriends into our home and he supports me in everything I do.

My story has a happy ending because my parents decided that it was their duty to put love above shame, even though that took effort, conscious learning and bucket loads of love.

10

WHAT IF YOUR FAMILY OR FRIENDS AREN'T SUPPORTIVE?

Wouldn't it be great if we lived in a world where this chapter wasn't necessary?

Where you could scream, "I'M A HOMO" at your school assembly and everyone would say, "Who cares? Sit down, you fool!" Unfortunately, we're not at that place just yet. When you come out, some people might react in a less than ideal way. Sometimes they'll just need time to get used to it. Sometimes you'll be able to educate them and win them over. But occasionally you might need to walk away.

ALMOST EVERY RELATIONSHIP IS SALVAGEABLE.

Some people are shocked when you come out because it changes their preconceived opinion of you. They might have imagined being a guest at your big, straight wedding. Now you've come along and ruined that. How selfish of you! The news that you're queer hits them like a tsunami. They feel confused, sad, panicky. What? Why? How? When?!

Know that this initial reaction may not be how they'll feel in the long term. Just look at my dad – he went from terrified and confused to loving and accepting in a matter of months, because he and I both took steps to restore our relationship. All you can do is be honest and open to questions, no matter how silly or hurtful they may seem.

WHAT IF THEY START TELLING ME I'M CONFUSED?

Confusion is a funny word. It's perfect for describing how you feel about long division, or the fact that you lose a single sock in every wash cycle. But if you have reached the point of coming out, you're probably not confused about your sexuality or gender identity any more. You've spent months or years agonizing over your thoughts and feelings. No one else can tell you how you feel. When you're hit with the "You must be confused" card, the best thing to do is calmly and assertively explain how confident you are about your sexuality or gender identity. Even if you're still questioning certain things, don't let that deter you. Describe the journey you've been on to bring you to this point. Even if that story takes hours, ask your friends or family to listen to you. Answer their questions. Challenge them, gently. Thrash it out a little.

Jason from Arizona remembers the difficult conversation he had with his grandmother:

"When I told her I was gay, she dismissed it as 'just a phase' and rolled her eyes. I felt like the years of figuring myself out were for nothing. A few days later I sat her down and asked if she had chosen her sexuality and to be attracted to Grandpa. She said no, but that the way she felt was 'normal'. I told her my feelings were normal too, and that being with a girl would be the most abnormal thing in the world. She didn't instantly come around, but I could tell she had heard me. Instead of fighting the news, she began asking questions and I was happy to slowly teach her."

In intense emotional situations, some people's natural reaction is to lash out in **anger**. You do not deserve to be treated badly. Be assertive and clear, but don't react to anger with anger. If you shout back, raise your voice or say hurtful things in retaliation, the situation might escalate. You might feel betrayed and hurt if someone reacts badly to your coming out, but remember, they may feel hurt and confused too.

If at any point you feel like your mental or physical health is in danger, reach out for help. Maybe there's a family member or friend you could stay with, or you could call an organization set up to care for LGBT+ young people like you. That might seem like a drastic move, but sometimes both sides can benefit from breathing space.

Remember: **You are not alone**. There are people waiting to help you in person, on the phone or online. Speaking to someone who understands your struggle is vital during a difficult time like this. Reach out to one of the organizations I've listed in the Help is Out There section of this book. You won't regret it.

There was a time when I believed coming out could land me on the streets, homeless. Thankfully that didn't happen because I had a supportive family and friends. Around a quarter of homeless people in the UK identify as LGBT+. You don't have to be part of that statistic. I have met many queer teens who were kicked out of home by parents who didn't support them but have since gone on to find a home, start amazing careers, make friends, fall in love and find happiness. No matter what happens, support is there for you and the future is bright.

Coming out is the first step towards a life where you get to be you, without acting or editing. Do it in your own time, do it with a plan in place in case things go wrong, and do it with your community by your side. We're cheering you on!

11

BEING THE ODD ONE OUT

Different. Bizarre. Weird. Original. Distinctive. Offbeat.

These all sound like great personality traits, don't they? The sort of qualities you look for in someone you'd like to be mates with, right? The problem is, when you're young, most people don't want to be different or weird or original. Most people want to fit in because offbeat people sometimes get laughed at. Teenagers are so judgemental!

Being gay instantly puts you into a minority – a wonderful minority, sure, but it automatically separates you from the mainstream. That's just a fact of life.

Just after I'd burst out of the closet, I wanted to talk about being gay all the time. I draped myself in rainbow-coloured clothes and I was practically singing musical theatre numbers in my sleep. Lots of baby gays do this – it's a right of passage, really. But a by-product of this newfound freedom was that I found myself being "othered" over and over by my family, friends and just about anyone else who knew me. By "othered" I mean I was made to feel like the odd one out. Were they doing it in a fun and friendly way? Probably. But to me, I knew this was a new normal that I was going to have to get used to.

For example, I was at a local barbecue when my mother's best friend welcomed me with a hug and twirled me around by my hand, saying

I looked "FAAAABULOUS darling!" And I was at Christmas dinner and my aunt made a joke that I wouldn't be able to open the jar of cranberry sauce (because the stereotype is that gay men are weak and effeminate). I think they were trying to show me that they were comfortable with my sexuality, but they were stereotyping me, and I soon grew tired of it. It made me feel like a one-dimensional homosexual character in a bad sitcom who's only there for light relief and cheap entertainment. I knew I had more to offer. I had interests, I had passions, I had opinions, I was more than my sexuality.

Since then, I've figured out ways to deal with the moments when I'm being "othered" by people who (mostly) mean well. I think these examples may come in handy for you, too, so here goes:

Generally, I laugh, smile and engage with the joke. Then I change the subject – "Oh how's the new job going?" "Are you going on holiday this summer?" I sometimes ask the person a deep and meaningful question and make it clear that I am interested in more than small talk (we all hate small talk, let's be honest!) or I might call them out on it, with a smile: "Wow, you're stereotyping me aren't you?"

It's also helpful to watch your own behaviour and make sure you're not othering *yourself* (unless you want to, of course!). Some gay people have a habit of making fun of themselves, getting in there first before anyone else can – that can be a result of being bullied when you were younger. But you're more than you're sexuality, and you deserve for other people to realize that, although you're proud of being gay, it doesn't define you. As you get older, people will start to think your sexuality is less of a big deal. Believe me, people will be SO disinterested in your gayness that you may begin to miss the attention!

Being the odd one out can seem like a negative at first, but as you get older, your sexuality will be the least interesting thing about you.

And one day you'll see that being special is often an advantage. Who wants to be the same as everyone else? Be proud of everything that makes you different!

Jake in Connecticut told me how he used the fact that he was the odd one out to his advantage:

"I was working at the perfume counter in my local mall. It was fun, but I really wanted to become an assistant manager in women's wear. I knew there were at least five other people going for this job so I had my work cut out for me.

I had done my research on the woman who interviewed me, and I found out that her best friend was a super camp gay dude who would come into the store and laugh with her by the customer service desk. This was my opportunity. I needed to let my gayness shine bright like a diamond!

Interview day came along, and I marched into that room with a big smile on my face and said, "Hey hun! Looking fab today". She smiled at me over her glasses and we began chatting about the role. When we were coming to the end of the interview, I mentioned that my boyfriend was cooking me dinner that night and I was preparing an outfit for Pride the following week. We ended up chatting nonsense and laughing about how bad our local gay bar is, and she offered me the job on the spot!

Do I feel bad that I used my sexuality to my favour? Not really! It felt like repayment for the years of hiding and changing myself for the benefit of other people. For the first time in my life, being the different one, the gay one, put me above the rest and got me the job I so badly wanted. I think I deserved it, to be honest."

12

BULLIES & HOW TO DEAL WITH THEM

"Things will get easier, people's minds will change, and you should be alive to see it." —*Ellen DeGeneres*

Bullies come in all shapes and sizes, with varying levels of aggression and different motivations for being awful to you or others. The one thing that's true for almost all bullies is that they have some underlying insecurity that they're desperately trying to hide, deflect attention from or ignore.

Understanding that not all bullies are inherently bad people is difficult. I mean, why would you smile at someone screaming "faggot" in your face? Why would you speak positively about a person who hit you for wearing a pink t-shirt? But if you take time to see the human emotions behind a bully's actions, you'll allow yourself to disconnect from the awful words and actions coming your way. Bullying feels personal, it feels malicious, it feels humiliating, but it's not about you, and it's not your fault. It's about the bully.

Understanding that not all bullies are inherently bad people is difficult.

Why do people bully others?

- Family problems
- Issues with anger management
- Internalized homophobia (they're scared of queer people because they're scared they might be queer)
- As an outlet for trauma or anger in another part of their life
- For attention
- Sheep behaviour (they're bullying because everyone else is doing it)
- They're bored
- They think it's funny and that you're in on the joke (they don't realize they're bullying you)
- They scared of people who are different from them.

Why me?!

You can become a bully's unlucky target for a number of reasons. In the war zone that is school, where hormones are gushing and everyone is desperately trying to fit in, any perceived difference in you is likely to be a gay rag to a homophobic bull!

A study carried out by anti-bullying organization Ditch The Label found that almost half of UK school students had experienced some kind of bullying but that only 14% felt that they had bullied someone in the past. These findings suggest that most bullies aren't aware that they are causing harm. They may feel they are just "having a laugh" at your expense. This is not okay. You deserve to feel happy, safe and comfortable in your skin wherever you are, especially in a place like school.

Again, if you're being bullied, IT IS NOT YOUR FAULT.

How can I stop it?

TALK TO YOUR BULLY

Tell them how they are making you feel, ask them why they are doing it and that you'd like them to stop. Remember, your bully is probably going through some difficult stuff in their life, too .

If your bully is likely to be violent, then avoid being alone with them.

ASK FOR HELP

The people who care about you most will want to protect you, but they can't do anything unless they know something is wrong. Find a teacher, family member or friend who you trust and tell them how the bullying is affecting you and that you need some help.

Tell your friends that if they see you being bullied they need to step in and ask the bully to stop – that's the true definition of safety in numbers!

IMPORTANT! Although it may seem like the safe option, try not to change who you are, how you walk, how you talk or how you dress to try and avoid being bullied. Faking it to fit in will only make you feel empty and unfulfilled. It's better to be yourself and make sure the bullying is monitored and stopped by your school, parents or friends.

Use common sense in certain situations where you may be alone or around a group of dangerous people. In this case keep yourself to yourself, don't provoke them and get away from them as quietly and quickly as you can.

WALK AWAY

Walk away – not just physically, but also emotionally. Actively try and practise letting hurtful words wash over you like water off a fabulous waterproof raincoat. Resist reacting when the bully targets you. They are trying to get a rise out of you. This reaction feeds them and may make the situation worse. If you ignore the bully and removing yourself from the situation, they might end up feeling silly and as if they have wasted their time and energy. They'll be less likely to pick on you again.

My all-time favourite response is to wait until they are done being nasty, leave a slight pause, and then crack a knowing smile and say, "Thank you, are you done now?". Your maturity and calmness may just rub off on them!

What to do about cyberbullying

There are loads of benefits to growing up in the digital age – you get to Facetime friends on the other side of the planet, stream endless episodes of *RuPaul's Drag Race* and stalk your crush on Instagram, imagining kissing his soft lips on a beach in Malibu while Miley Cyrus plays in the background and the sea mist caresses your faces... Oh, just me? Okay.

But most good things have a dark side. I'm talking about cyberbullying. It's probably the worst kind of emotional abuse because it follows you everywhere and can pop up at any time, day or night.

I was 16 when I first experienced cyberbullying. Every day, people left tormenting messages on my YouTube videos.

"Shut up, you disgusting fag."

"I know where you live. I'm going to get you."

I was young, new to the internet and afraid, and these bullies drove

CYBERBULLYING TOP TIPS:

- Take screenshots of the messages, images or videos
- Don't respond to them
- Block the bully's account
- Report the harassment on their account
- Speak to a family member, friend, or teacher about it
- Reach out to one of the anti-bullying organizations listed at the back of this book.

me off YouTube for seven years. The site had given me a voice, a place to express my creativity, a place I could meet people like me. But those keyboard warriors silenced me with intimidation. In reality, they didn't know where I lived, they weren't going to get me, and calling me a fag means nothing. It's just a word. It hurt, yes, but I knew deep down that I was a good person and that I was surrounded by people who loved me. It took many years of learning how to love myself, my gayness, my voice and all the things the trolls hated about me to finally NOT CARE. I now care so little that I use mean comments in videos for a giggle with my friends or parents.

Your haters, your bullies, your trolls do not define you. Their words aren't about you, their actions are not motivated by you and if they're targeting of you, it's not your fault. When you're being bullied, it can feel like there's no way out and that nobody wants to help. But that's not true. Speak up and reach out for help, and you'll get it. Things get better, bullies lose interest, people move schools and with age even the most awful bullies grow out of their terrible behaviour. As my mother always told me when things were overwhelming – "This too shall pass".

13

SEXUALITY & FAITH

"Can God really love me if I'm gay?"

This is a question that plagues lots of LGBT+ people of faith and their families. It's a worry that leads to people living secret double lives, seeking damaging gay conversion therapy and at times, being excommunicated from their family and religious community. But it doesn't have to be this way.

A couple of years ago, I made a documentary series called *Queer Britain* for the BBC (which you can watch on the BBC Three YouTube channel). During filming, I had the opportunity to meet queer people who identify as Muslim, Christian, Jehovah's Witness and Sikh. Almost all of them felt a close connection to their faith, yet struggled to find a harmonious way to live an authentic faith-led life that allowed them to express their sexuality without shame.

Elijah is one of the people I interviewed on *Queer Britain*. He's a Christian pansexual trans man who struggled to reconcile his faith with his sexuality and gender identity but he eventually found a church who embraced him for who he is.

"I had the feeling that I was somehow wrong or that I was a bit gross. I felt isolated and sad all the time. But the knowledge that

there was a power that loved me, no matter what I did or who I was, actually saved my life. The church that I'm part of now practises what they preached in terms of solidarity with the LGBT+ community, so I always felt safe."

What Elijah found in his congregation is special but not totally unusual. There are faith groups all over the world that open their arms to the LGBT+ community.

When I joined Elijah at his church I could feel a tangible warmth and togetherness from people of all ages and backgrounds. As Elijah went through his naming ceremony, where he officially declared his new identity as a man before his god, I was blown away with how the church embraced him. The congregation gave him a standing ovation, cheering, clapping, hugging him and offering him endless encouragement. As a former Irish Catholic, this was something I had never experienced and it brought me to tears.

Soon after I came out, Dad dropped Islam, and Mom and I dropped Catholicism. We turned to Humanism, the belief that people, love and science are the centre of the universe. Why? At the time we thought it would be hypocritical to follow faiths that seemed, for the most part, to be anti-LGBT+. But since then I've learned a thing or two.

Sure, we might be told that the dude in the sky doesn't like gay people, but what we forget is that it's not god telling us this – it's other people. A faith is a personal connection with something greater than you. Of course this can be celebrated, learned and expressed as a group, but it starts with YOU.

The nature of most belief systems means that they're pretty damn old, like REALLY old – about as ancient as *Drag Race* Season 1. As-

There are faith groups all over the world that open their arms to the LGBT+ community.

pects of a religion naturally change over time but the holy books stay the same. Some scriptures may lead you to believe that homosexuality is a sin, but with time, society changes and so does the way religious leaders interpret the meaning of holy texts. Whatever religion you are, you'll probably find a community that teaches love and acceptance for all. A quick Google search of your faith, location and the letters LGBT+ will bring up a list of wonderful faith organizations that may be the perfect fit for you.

There are always going to be homophobic, biphobic, transphobic people in the world, and some of them will use their religion as an excuse for their views. But if your faith is important to you, you can seek out a community where you are valued as an equal, where people love you and celebrate you for who you are.

Simon-Anthony Rhoden

Simon-Anthony Rhoden was born in London. He trained as an actor at the Italia Conti school and LAMDA, and he's currently playing Lola, the lead, in West End musical *Kinky Boots*.

Growing up within the Caribbean culture where it just wasn't okay to be gay, I found it so difficult to be my authentic self. And so I would do anything to get people to like me – make jokes, run errands, compromise my happiness, all in order to distract from my big secret. By as I got older, I learned that people-pleasing had stunted my growth as a person and realized that, I wasn't really making my own decisions – I was doing things to appease others. There's nothing wrong with making other people happy, but only if it doesn't compromise your own happiness. I think it's important for young people, especially young people dealing with LGBTQ+ issues, to find their own voices and start experimenting with them as soon as they can. I've learned that not everyone is going to like me, regardless of my sexuality, and that's fine.

The advice I would give my 16-year-old self is "Be your most authentic self and make your own choices." As Oscar Wilde said: "Be yourself; everyone else is already taken."

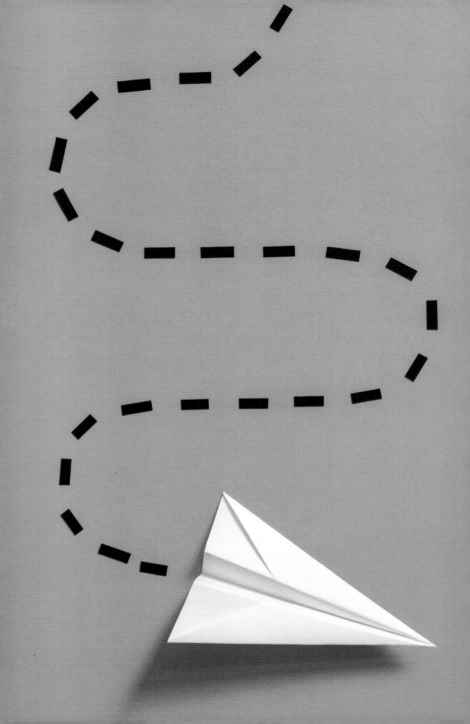

14

FROM MY FAMILY TO YOURS

Coming out is pretty tough, I think we can all agree on that. We've usually had a long time to reflect on our feelings and identity before telling the ones we love who we really are.

When your family finds out you're queer, it can hit them like a ton of bricks and that's no surprise, really. After all, they are hearing the news for the first time and they are expected to get it and shower you with acceptance right away. In reality, they might need time to process the news and work on their perception of what it means to have an LGBT+ person in the family.

This chapter is written by my parents for your friends and family. I've asked them to answer the questions they get asked most often by people who have just found out that their child is gay, bi or trans. My parents went through a long period of adjustment while trying to figure out how to accept and love me for who I am. They eventually realized that me being gay didn't actually change anything and that I was the same son as I had always been. The only difference was that I was now free to express myself without fear or shame and that they would be needed for many Pride parades!

My kid just came out to me. What should I do?

MOM: It may feel like the child you brought into the world and reared with love has completely changed. They haven't. This is still your beautiful kid who needs your support and understanding – now more than ever before.

It has likely taken them a long, long time to come to a place where they are confident enough to share this news with you, so listen to them carefully. Without being too honest about your feelings, support them and let the news sink in before reacting too strongly.

It's okay to ask questions and to feel confused. Be respectful. Don't blame anyone for the news you've just heard and try to hear your child out as they answer.

Make sure your child has no doubt in their mind that you love them unconditionally and that you'll keep the news to yourself if they ask you to. Right now, your job is to let your child feel heard. This is a major moment in both your lives. Try to make it one that you'll both look back on with fond memories.

When you have time to yourself, allow the news to sink in and seek help or advice from family, friends, a therapist or an LGBT+ support group, many of which offer services to parents of newly "out" teens.

Did I do something wrong as a parent to make my child this way?

DAD: You haven't done anything wrong. I believed this myself for a while, too – that I hadn't put enough masculinity into him when he was a kid or that I had slipped up as a father in some way. This is not true.

Your child's sexuality is not a choice, and it's not influenced by how they were brought up or what they were exposed to. It's in their genetics, just as being heterosexual is in mine. It was there from before birth, just like their eye and hair colour.

Accept that your parenting – good or bad – had no affect on who your child is sexually attracted to. If anything, it's a compliment to your parenting that your child has the bravery to confide in you. Don't let that bravery be for nothing. Show them love, and communicate your feelings carefully, so that you don't hurt them.

How can I support my child?

MOM: First and most importantly, be a listening ear for them. If you're the first parent they've told and they're not ready for the other parent to hear the news, then respect that. They will do it in their own time.

Seek out other parents (like us) who have been through the coming out journey. They may be distant family friends, work colleagues or people you've found through a local LGBT+ support group. They will make this experience feel less daunting and will likely give you tips on how to calmly and encouragingly support your child.

It's more important now than ever to shower your child with love. They will be extremely sensitive to anything you say or do in the weeks after they come out. This is normal! They will be looking for a sign that they made the right decision in telling you. Assure them through regular verbal expressions of affection that they did the right thing. A few hugs and kisses won't go amiss (if you're anything like us)!

But what will our family, friends, neighbours think?

DAD: As my wife, Lorraine said to me when Riyadh came out: *"Sam, stop worrying about what other people think. This is your son, your blood. When you're on your deathbed thinking about what you have achieved in your life, it will be your children who are by your side kissing you and telling you that they love you. The only thing that matters is the four of us. Family first."*

Ultimately, who cares what anyone outside your family thinks? They will have to learn to love and accept your child, otherwise it's their loss. It may take time for those in your social or family circle to come around to the news, but that's their job, not yours, and certainly not your kid's.

Surely this is just a phase? Shouldn't help my child "see the light"?

MOM: I don't think your child would have made the difficult decision to come out if what they were feeling was a mere phase. This is something that they have been feeling and potentially struggling with silently for a very long time.

Do not try to change them or talk them out of it. This is not comparable to a discussion of what piercing or tattoo they want to get – their sexuality or gender identity is a deep, unchangeable aspect of who they are. Asking them to alter it would be like asking a person of colour to become white. It's impossible for them to change, and deeply offensive to ask them to.

Let time heal you, them and your relationship. Let this also be a chance for you to discover who your child really is, in a new, unfiltered and fearless way.

Think back to the way your child was when they were young. You might remember hints that they were different. It'll probably become clear to you that they were queer right from the start.

I'm finding this news hard to handle. How can I get support without hurting my child's feelings?

DAD: As Lorraine said, time is an amazing healer and a way for you to get clarity on what really matters. Honestly, you'll look back and wonder what on Earth you were worried about.

Talking is what helped me figure it all out. Specifically, talking to another father who had two gay sons. Without judgement, he told me that my feelings and fears were exactly the same as the ones he'd experienced. I was able to ask all the difficult questions that were too sensitive to ask Riyadh directly. It helped a lot.

Is my child's life going to be different or difficult now that they're out of the closet and LGBT+?

MOM: Yes, their life is likely to be different but not necessarily in a bad way.

We always fear as parents that our children may be judged or ridiculed in some way. This may happen, but at least now that you know, you'll be able to help, protect or listen to them if it happens. They're no longer fighting this battle on their own.

And things are going to change for you, too. You'll be able to see how enlightening, loving and fun the LGBT+ community is. This is something I now realize is the greatest gift I could have asked for. I am so blessed to have a gay son in my life. Because of him, our minds and hearts have been opened.

15

BEING AN ALLY

If you're reading this, you're probably a friend, family member or classmate of an LGBT+ person. First of all, thank you! You care enough to find out how you can support the lesbian, gay, bi, trans or queer person (or people) in your life.

Being an ally means more than watching a few episodes of *Will & Grace* with your gay bestie on a Saturday night while you exchange stories about hot guys on Instagram.

To be a true ally you have to consciously do your best to support not

just one LGBT+ person but an entire community by learning about their struggles, celebrating their triumphs and challenging homophobic or transphobic behaviour whenever you see it in person, in legislation or online (making sure you put your physical safety first at all times).

The queer community has made incredible leaps and bounds towards equality in recent years, but this couldn't have been achieved without army of allies rallying around and pushing for laws to change, for LGBT+ people to be elected, and for bigoted voices to be silenced with education and love. So what I'm saying is thanks, and we need you now more than ever.

Queer young people are still three times more likely to attempt suicide than their heterosexual counterparts. Conservative leaders around the world are trying to roll back the clock on equality measures that were decades in the making, and homophobic hate crimes are steadily on the rise in major cities like London and New York.

How to be a good ally

- Become aware of the daily microaggressions faced by the LGBT+ community – people saying things like "That's so gay!" or laughing at gay love scenes in movies for instance – and call it out when you see it happening

- Speak to your LGBT+ friends, family members and work colleagues about what bothers them most and what you could do to make things easier for them

- Get involved in protests for equal rights

- Attend pride marches with LGBT+ friends and socialize with them outside Pride season.

- Try to educate older members of your family about the LGBT+ community and why it's important to support them

- Do the same with the young people you know, including your children. They are the next generation of allies and LGBT+ people. Teaching them to accept and love all people, no matter who they are or who they love, is an invaluable a life lesson.

- Support LGBT+ charities and organizations by volunteering, campaigning or fundraising. There's a list of organizations in the Useful Contacts Section at the end of this book.

Being a queer ally

So you identify on the queer spectrum and want to make sure you are there for your LGBT+ brothers/sisters/siblings? That's great!

You are in the special position of knowing exactly what it feels like to be a minority and what good and bad things can happen as a result of that. Remember that our community is only strong when we are speaking as one, acting as one and constantly demanding equal treatment.

I think queer people have a duty to be allies. The queer community that we were born into desperately needs every one of us to speak up and push for positive change. That's why it hurts me when I hear a gay man say he hates feminine gay men, or that it's unnatural for two people of the same sex to get married or have children. Statements like this come from internalized homophobia, but they can cause so much harm to others in the community. It's important to remember that, even within the queer community, some people have an easier time than others.

People at the intersection of race, disability, gender identity, sex and sexuality are the ones who need to be supported and shouted for the most. If you don't understand what I mean, think about a black, disabled, transgender lesbian. She faces racism, ableism, transphobia, homophobia AND sexism. That's a lot more than I have to deal with. Recognizing the privilege you have because of your race, sex, gender identity, etc is always a good first step.

If you don't know where to start, turn to the Useful Contacts section and look up one of the brilliant LGBT+ organizations working in your area. See how you can get involved, and help make the world a better place for all of us!

Recognizing the privilege you have because of your race, sex, gender identity, etc is always a good first step.

16

MY FIRST PRIDE

The first time I found my community was at my first ever Pride in Dublin.

I was 16 and had lied to my parents about where I was going. My best friend and I headed into the city and found a sea of brightly coloured, loud and proud people. Thousands of them were smiling, hugging, kissing, dancing and having a great time without a care in the world. There was no judgement or fear in the air. We were strong together. This was a first for me and I was instantly addicted.

My friend and I marched nervously with the crowds through the streets of the capital before stopping at a public park for a finale show and speeches by key LGBT+ figures. It felt as though the march was a religious pilgrimage and this was the climax – like the gay pope was about to arrive and bless us with her glittering homo glory.

I sat and watched as a famous drag queen named Panti Bliss took the stage to a thunderous applause. In an impassioned speech that would have rivalled Martin Luther King, she told

There was no judgement or fear in the air. We were strong together.

us what the word "community" meant. I sat there, a little baby gay, tears rolling down my face. I felt part of something bigger than me. I felt like I mattered to these people and they mattered to me, and for the first time in my life I felt **proud**.

I somehow found an ancient grainy recording of the speech online and these were Panti's exact words.

"We are gathered here today to celebrate who we are and how far we have come. Today we stand here as a community, strong, powerful, vibrant and PROUD!

We have much to feel proud of ourselves about today, but at the same time, I want more! I will continue to want more until each and every one of us, from the butchest lesbian to the femmiest gay can walk the streets of this city, any street, any hour of the day or night, free from the fear of harassment or intimidation. I want MORE!

I will continue to want more until this state recognizes our relationships under the law; not just accepts our relationships but cherishes our relationships as they cherish the relationships of our heterosexual brothers and sisters.

These things that we want are not gay rights, because the truth is, there's no such thing as gay rights, there are only RIGHTS."

(I'm not crying, you are, leave me alone.)

What does the LGBT+ community mean to you?

I asked my Twitter followers what the LGBT+ community means to them. Here are some of the Tweets I received.

A usually/hopefully safe and non-judgemental space/group of people where you can talk openly and unashamedly about being LGBT+ and your experiences, and find support. I've found my community online, mostly, but also within my IRL friendship groups.

As a person living in rural Ireland, my community are my queer friends. We hold each other up and make each other laugh and just understand things about one another that nobody else would.

The queer community means knowing you're not alone. Knowing there are others like you, and that they're doing okay. It's a place to discover role models, connect and enjoy queer culture. I found my community on the internet first and in real life later.

To me, community means everyone being there for each other, supporting one another and having fun. It's having somewhere to go for advice or help, and having a large support network of people who understand you. It's somewhere to go for help, comfort or validation. It's fantastic and has helped me lots.

It's the chosen family we sometimes love more than our own family. Yes, we have certainly fought our battles but in the end we are all rooting for each other and have a genuine love for one another.

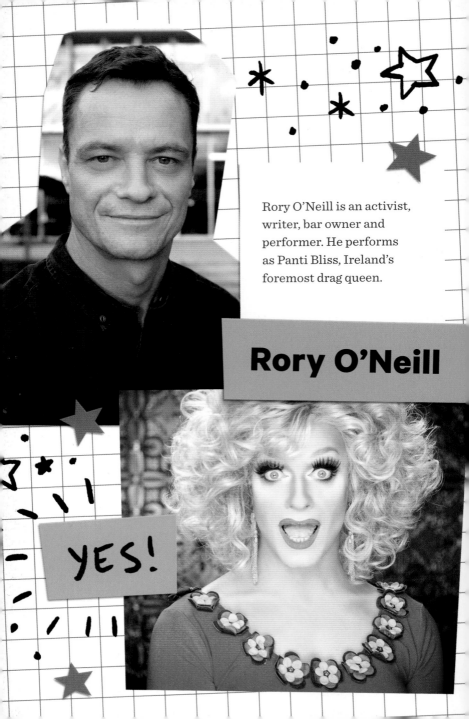

Rory O'Neill is an activist, writer, bar owner and performer. He performs as Panti Bliss, Ireland's foremost drag queen.

Rory O'Neill

YES!

Dear 16-year-old me,

I know. Grown ups are annoying – always telling you that things aren't as bad as you think and that one day you'll look back and blah blah blah. And you're right. We are annoying, because what use is "Blah blah blah, one day" to you now? Not much, I'm afraid. And what's worse is, here I am about to do the "Blah blah" thing to you and I can only imagine how annoying it is to find out that you've become one of those annoying adults yourself. Ugh! But, there you go. Life is weird.

*And you'd know, because, well, you're kinda weird. Yes you are! And you know it. But here's the really weird bit: being weird is a **good** thing! I promise. You'll just have to trust me on that. So try not to worry or stress too much about the things that make you feel awkward and different and out-of-place at the moment, because (and again you'll just have to trust me on this) over time those same things will become the **very** things that make you special and unique, and will become the very things that I, and others, will come to value and cherish most about you. And you can't change who you are even if you want to, so be you – because there is no one else like you. You have abilities and talents that are unique to you, and they are valuable and important. And one day, (blah blah blah ☺), people will see that. You have a lot to offer.*

Oh, and while I have you: your spots will clear up and you are hotter than you think you are. I swear! Turns out that youth is attractive in itself. I know! Weird, right? But it's true, so start hitting on hotter guys.

x Old Rory

Finding friends, finding love.

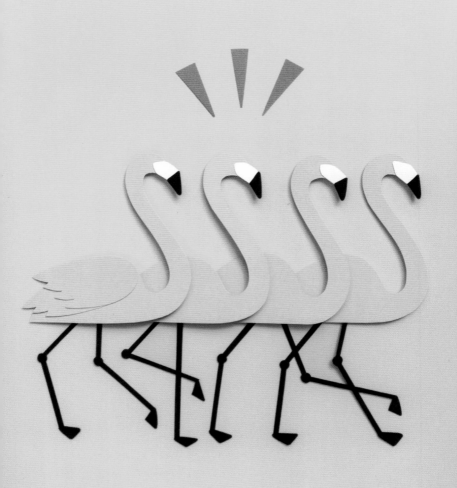

17

FINDING YOUR TRIBE

Community this, community that... WHERE is this community we hear so much about?

Is it in a rainbow-lined village with rainbow roads, rainbow trees and rainbow dogs? Is there a welcome party? Do you get a membership card when you come out? Well, it's not quite as glam as that, but your tribe is out there waiting for you!

Navigating the world after coming out (to yourself or other people) can be daunting, but one of the biggest rewards is a

It's an incredible feeling to travel the world knowing that wherever you go, you'll find people who are just like you.

global family of people who get you and love you just the way you are. It's a brotherhood and sisterhood made up of hundreds of millions of LGBT+ people –ready-made friends, a chosen family, an army of supporters. If you've experienced the pain of being rejected by your family, friends or school mates because of your sexuality or gender identity, your LGBT+ family will mean even more to you.

I'm often surprised by the incredible closeness that exists across borders within the LGBT+ community. It's an incredible feeling to travel the world knowing that wherever you go, you'll find people who are just like you. Whether I meet a gay couple in a restaurant or a trans person on the beach, or I stumble across a drag show at a local dingy gay bar, I know that I'll be met with a familiar warmth, welcome and connection. There have been times when I've bumped into queer people I've never met, and within minutes we're chatting away like friends who've known each other for years. It's as if the queer community has a language that's made up of intonation, body language, humour and empathy as well as words. It's hard to describe, but trust me, it's magical.

I interviewed Josh, a former Jehovah's Witness, who was kicked out of his church and home when his family discovered he was gay. His parents cut off contact with him almost immediately. Although it's a sad story, Josh found the love and support he needed in London's queer community:

"I found people here now that have become my new family, that have taken me under their wing, that have made friends with me and said, 'Look, Josh, if you need us at any time, we're here for you'. And I think it's really important to have that support because I still need to carry on figuring myself out."

Before you come out, the world can fell quite isolating and cold. But know that you have millions and millions of people waiting to welcome you into one of the most loving communities you could imagine.

How do I find friends?

and maybe more?

Social Media

In a time before social media – Okay, yes, I am THAT old – it was difficult to find your tribe. Thankfully today it's much easier to find your people and build friendships that could last a lifetime. But how do you find them? Be social!

- Find YouTube videos on LGBT+ topics and get chatting to (nice) people in the comments

- Search for specific hashtags like #YAYYOUREGAY on Twitter and Instagram where you can connect with other people interested in this book, queer TV or news stories

- Follow some LGBT+ activists and celebrities. Thousands of other young queer people follow and interact with them too

- Create a video or blog talking about your experiences, hobbies and life. Ask people to contact you with their own stories and build connections

- If you're comfortable to do it, perhaps add a rainbow flag to your Twitter or Instagram bio so other people can find you

- Share, post about or retweet LGBT+ content that interests you and start a conversation with people about it

- Ask a friend to connect you with other LGBT+ people they know.

Real Life The internet isn't the only way to make fabulous friends. You can also find them IRL. (Wow, how old skool!)

||||||||||||||||||||||||||||||||||||||||||||||||||||||||||||||||||||||||||||||||||||||||||||||||||||||||||||||

- Seek out LGBT+ social groups, youth groups, local events and talks. Some of these organize social gatherings.

- Look out for LGBT+ meet ups for people who are into the same things as you. Maybe there's a queer orchestra or choir where you live, or a monthly meet up for gay gamers.

- If you've already come out to friends at school, as if they have any LGBT+ pals they can introduce you to.

- Pride marches, protests and rallies for LGBT+ rights are great places to meet like-minded people.

Like any big group of people who have one main thing in common, the LGBT+ community is very diverse, and it's far from perfect. In fact we have A LOT to work on. We can be racist, we can body shame, we can leave people out, and we can even be homophobic and transphobic. But we're constantly learning and changing, and each new generation of queers that joins us brings new ways of thinking with them. Yes, that's you!

So do your gay big brother a favour and be kind to your own kind. Speak from the heart and fight for what you know is right. Challenge hurtful or divisive behaviour and be the change you want to see in your community, because it's just that: yours.

> **So do your gay big brother a favour and be kind to your own kind.**

18

STAYING SAFE ONLINE

**"It's a jungle out there, kid."
Someone once told me
that. I don't remember
who. Or maybe it's from
a movie. Actually, I
think I made it up. It
doesn't matter.**

The internet is amazing for dating, connecting with people, building friendships, entertaining and educating yourself, but it can also be a dangerous place for a young gay dude. I don't want to sound like I'm nagging, but listen up: I am your gay big brother, after all. BE CAREFUL when chatting to strangers online, especially if you plan to meet someone in person. It's important to remember that not everyone out there has the best intentions. Here are a few tips on how to stay safe online, whatever you're getting up to.

Dating apps

DON'T USE THEM IF YOU'RE UNDER 18
Age limits are there for a reason – you have no idea who you're talking to when you're chatting on an app, so put your safety first.

PROTECT YOUR PERSONAL INFO

Only put basic information on your profile. Never share your exact location, where you go to school or where you work, your full name, phone number or bank details. (Seems obvious, but I have to say it!)

Is he who he says he is?

If someone claims to be a cute 18-year-old named Kyle who's into rock climbing and long walks on the beach (who still says that?) then get them to prove it.

VIDEO CALL

Even the most elaborate and professional of catfish can't fake their identity on a Facetime chat. If you ask them to chat and they say no over and over again, end the conversation and DO NOT meet up with them.

PHOTO CHALLENGE

If he is too shy to go on video call, then ask him to pose for a pic that he couldn't possibly steal from someone else's profile. You could ask him to take a selfie holding a specific message written on a piece of paper, to make a particular hand signal or a pose with an object like a clock reading an exact time. This may sound silly but try to have fun with it.

Catfishing

verb • when a person creates a fake identity on social media in order to deceive people, perhaps for attention, bullying or as a scam.

NUDES

There will come a point in your online life when a guy will ask you to send him a nude pic of yourself, or will send you one of himself. If you receive a nude that you didn't ask for and it makes you feel uncomfortable, then block the person right away and report the profile if you feel you need to.

If you feel the urge to share an intimate picture with someone, here are some things to consider first:

- **How well do you know them?** Nobody can be trusted to keep a nude image of you to themselves, no matter how well you know or trust them. Every time you think about sending an image, imagine your friends or family seeing that image and think about how that would make you feel. It sounds dramatic, but believe me, it happens!

- **If you do decide to send a nude:** DO NOT SHOW YOUR FACE. This also goes for identifiable birthmarks, scars, posters on your bedroom wall, furniture or anything that could help someone trace the picture back to you.

- **Are you being pressured into sending a nude?** You should never let someone persuade you to do something you're not comfortable doing – and some catfish have been known to get a compromising image of a person and then use it as blackmail.

- **How old are you?** Depending on where you live in the world, the images you send to another person may actually constitute child pornography and be illegal. This could get you or the person who receives the image in a lot of trouble!

Online hate

Trolls, homophobes, bullies, haters – whatever you call them, you don't have time for horrible people in your life! You've got some fabulosity to be getting on with.

As a young gay guy on YouTube, way back when the Internet was just becoming popular, I was subjected to a lot of daily abuse. The nasty comments ranged from mean names to threats that someone was going to "get" me. The trolls were just trying to scare me because I was young, confident and unapologetically myself, but still, they managed to drive me away from my creative safe space on YouTube for seven years! I want to make sure that never happens to anyone else.

We are all in this together. Whether you're being hated on, or you see it happening to someone else, it's our collective job to call it out when it's safe to do so, or report the harmful content to the website.

If you feel upset or scared because of what's being said to you online, ask for help right away. Don't wait. Speak to a friend, teacher, school counsellor, family member or a helpline (see the help section at the back of this book). Telling someone what's going on will help you take action to stop what's going on and remind you that you're not alone.

In the darkest moments when I was being abused online, I really felt like these people had found something in me that they truly hated and found disgusting. In reality, many online bullies attack others as a way of processing anger over something bad happening in **their** life. They may even be struggling with their own sexuality or gender identity. So although it sounds crazy clichéd, try not to take their words personally. A faceless person typing nonsense behind an anonymous profile should never take away your freedom to be 100% YOU.

19

GOING OUT

Being part of a global online queer community is great and all, but there's nothing like actually getting out there, being face-to-face with people who are just like you and feeling that close bond that exists in every gay bar and club around the world.

Being in a gay bar is special for me. I'll never forget the moment I walked into The George in Dublin for the first time. I just knew it was a wild, colourful and hedonistic safe space and that I'd spend a lot of time there in the future, socializing and learning about queer culture.

Going out to bars and clubs is fun – but they're for over-18s only. And let's be honest, if you go out on the gay scene, you'll come across alcohol and drugs, and you need to have your wits about you.

> **Going out to bars and clubs is fun – but they're for over-18s only.**

Being an Irish chap means that I know a thing or two about drinking and bars. So listen up:

- Always respect the door policy. If you're underage you could get in serious trouble or put the bar in trouble with the authorities for having someone underage in their building

- If you're legally allowed to drink and are planning to have alcohol, then make sure you've had a nice big meal with plenty of carbs. Drinking on an empty stomach is never a good idea.

- Have a pint of water in between drinks. Not only will it keep you hydrated, hangover-free and able to keep on dancing, it will also save you money!

- Try to stay out of drink rounds. People drink at different paces and if one person in a round of six people is drinking twice as fast as everyone else, you'll feel pressure to consume alcohol faster just to keep up

- It can be easy to lose friends in a big club, so when you get in, decide on a meeting point where you will go if you get separated

- Never leave a club alone or with somebody you don't know.

- Keep your phone, wallet and keys in your front pockets, never your back pockets. You'd be surprised how easily someone can take your stuff as they rub against you on the dance floor

- Do me a favour and pay to put your coat into the cloakroom. In the decade that I've been frequenting gay bars, I've had four jackets stolen from chairs. It's much more expensive to buy a new coat than to pay for the cloakroom.

Drugs

Don't do them! The end.

That's what your mother would say but I'm not your mother. Of course my advice is to stay away from drugs – but I need to explain why.

Your health is more important than following the crowd, so don't risk it.

Drugs are unregulated and they're passed around and sold illegally, so there's no way of knowing what is actually in the pill, powder, liquid or joint you are being offered. Even if you see other people taking a substance and having a great time, it's still really risky. Different people can react differently to the same substance, and drugs can contain ingredients that might unknowingly be allergic to or that might react badly with any medication you're taking.

If you or a friend takes a substance and you feel worried, call an ambulance immediately and tell staff at the bar or club what's going on.

Peer pressure may make you feel like a loser for not taking drugs. Ignore this. Your health is more important than following the crowd, so don't risk it.

Other ways to go out

If you're under 18, you won't be able to go to gay bars and clubs. And anyway, plenty of LGBT+ people prefer to socialize in other ways. There are so many different LGBT+ groups, clubs and societies where you can meet friends and hang out with like-minded people. Google and see what's available near you – maybe there will be an LGBT+ youth group, a lesbian choir, a gay orchestra, a trans swimming club...

DIFFERENT KINDS OF RELATIONSHIPS

Remember when you used to read fairytales? Guy meets girl, girl falls in love with guy, they get married, have kids and live happily ever after?

Some people really do have relationships like that – but there's no rule that says you have to commit to one person for the rest of your life. Monogamy (being with one person, and not having sex with anyone else) doesn't suit everyone. And some people don't like being in relationships at all. On the opposite page, you'll see some different kinds of relationships. Your relationship does not have to fit into one of these categories (or any others). So long as you and the other person/people are honest and respectful of each other, and you're both happy, you're on the right track, baby.

By the way, being in a monogamous relationship DOES NOT MAKE YOU BORING. Some cool kids out there would have you believe otherwise, but take it from me: if it works for you both, then rock on, be happy and love one another.

> **Your relationship does not have to fit into one of these categories (or any others).**

Common kinds of romantic relationships

Single
Someone who isn't involved in a serious relationship with anyone

Monogamous
A couple who don't have sex with other people

Open
A couple who are open to having sex or relationships with people outside their relationship

Monogamish
A term made popular by writer Dan Savage. This is when a couple agrees that they can occasionally kiss or have sex with others outside of the relationship, as long as they follow certain rules

Polyamory
When someone has several romantic and/or sexual relationships at the same time. They might have one main partner and other more casual partners, or they might not have one main partner at all. All involved will usually know and agree to this arrangement

Throuple/Triad
A polyamorous relationship between three people. They may have three-way dates, live together in the same house, and sleep in the same bed

21

FIRST DATES

Meeting a complete stranger in a random bar/café/restaurant and spending hours doing a "job interview" for the position of boyfriend is daunting for anyone.

But if you go into a date with an optimistic and carefree frame of mind, it'll be way more enjoyable. Ask yourself what's the worst that can happen? Even if there's no spark at all, having a real conversation with another person is great experience, and you'll find the whole experience so much easier the next time.

You may feel awkward as hell, but remember the hottie you're with will be feeling nervous too, so if it breaks the ice, just say how you're feeling! The worst that can happen is that you'll both laugh it off.

Don't pretend to be someone you're not, or that you like things you don't like, just to impress a guy. You might get a second date, but do you really want to be with someone you can't relax around? Be yourself and have fun. There's nothing more magical than finding someone you genuinely click with.

There's nothing more magical than finding someone you genuinely click with.

WHERE TO GO ON A FIRST DATE

Choose a place where there's plenty going on that you can talk about, so you avoid those awkward silences we all hate. You could pick a place neither of you have been so you can enjoy it together for the first time. If it's summertime, do something outdoors. There's nothing like fresh air and open spaces to spark romance.

Lots of people go to the theatre or cinema on a first date, but I think that's a bad idea – you have to be quiet, so you can't talk and get to know each other. I'd also avoid clubs, where there'll be loads of other guys. You want to be the focus of this date!

Good first date places	Bad first date places
• Restaurant, café or bar	• Cinema
• Concert – only if you're standing and you can talk	• Theatre
• Fairground	• Graveyard – bit of a downer
• A walk with a destination (café, bar, mini-golf etc)	• A walk with no destination
• Botanical gardens	• Nightclub

SAFETY

Meeting a random dude you came across online comes with a whole host of risks. Loads of guys lie about their height (I know this because I'm a shorty and I'm guilty of this!), but he might be lying about other things too. So make sure you follow the safety suggestions on pages 99-101 before you go on your date.

My first date with Josh

The day of my first date with my now boyfriend, Josh, I wasn't feeling it. I was tired, I had loads of work to do and it just felt like an EFFORT. Thank god I ignored all of that and went!

The date came about in a completely unconventional way. My friend Calum had gone on a date with Josh a couple of weeks earlier. They had a nice evening, but there was no romantic spark between them. Again, thank god for that!

Calum, who's an intuitive guy, had a feeling that my personality and Josh's would be a good match. He quietly suggested to both of us that we should meet.

I knew of Josh because we had been following (and thirsting) after each other on Instagram for a few months but the chats had been limited to a couple of cringe exchanges in DMs.

The minute I got to the date (I was ten minutes late, as I am for everything), the chemistry was flying! Moral of the story: even if it seems like a lot of effort, push yourself and go on that date. You may just meet the one!

Hey Riyadh!
Just wanted to say hey!
Really nice profile! I defo think I've seen you at an event or two 😄 Really nice channel!
Have a good week!
Josh x

Hey Josh, same to you! Lovely pics with Cal recently. He was telling me how fun it was to shoot with you. Next time we're at the same event we need to catch up in person 😜 x

Yeah he's so lovely. For sure will come say hey! X

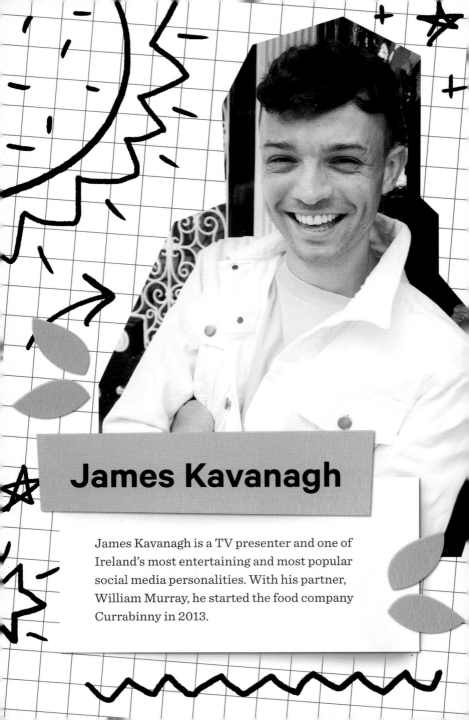

James Kavanagh

James Kavanagh is a TV presenter and one of Ireland's most entertaining and most popular social media personalities. With his partner, William Murray, he started the food company Currabinny in 2013.

Hey twink James, it's zaddy James here. Lol, I wish I were a zaddy – I basically still have your 16-year-old body. Soz about that – you don't love the gym. Right now, you're going through hell. I've been there, literally. But know that all of this homophobia and bullying you're experiencing is going to make you a tough and empathetic bitch when you get to my age. I know you don't have great friends now, and you really want them, but very soon you'll be inundated with them. You're going to get to kiss loads of hot boys and go to loads of parties. Lots and lots of parties. I know right now it seems like being gay is a curse, but one day you'll realize that being gay is a total joy and a gift. So keep your head up: you're heading for happiness – real soon.

22

FIRST KISS

Kissing is gross and fascinating all at the same time.

Scientists say it's a way for us to determine if a potential mate is a genetic match through smell, taste and touch. We are some of the only creatures in the world to practise kissing in a romantic/sexual way, yet we don't really know how it became popular. Kissing isn't a global thing, either. Only 46% of the world's population do it on the reg.

Most gay guys have two "first kisses": One with a girl, which is more like a dress rehearsal (sorry hun!) and then a first kiss with another guy, the main event, which is usually filled with fireworks, butterflies and a pounding heart full of passion.

Your first kiss is one you'll never forget. It'll likely be wet and messy with the addition of a sore jaw, clashing teeth and awkward head movements. But soon you'll be smooching like they do in the movies. At least that's what I was going for – think Jack and Rose from *Titanic* in the back of a vintage car vibes.

There's no right or wrong way to kiss, but it always helps to slow down, be gentle and try to flow in the direction of the other person, not against it. Kissing isn't a competition, it's a team sport.

My first kiss was with a girl named Julianne at a teenage disco in Dublin. Her friend confidently paraded over to me and asked if I'd kiss her. "Sure, which one is she?" I asked as I nervously scanned the packed sweaty dance floor. She was pretty and didn't look like she'd destroy me with her mouth. "Okay, let's do this, Riyadh," I thought. "You're already about a year behind your friends.".

On the outside, I was oozing charisma, confidence and cockiness, but on the inside, I was terrified. What if she knows I'm a first timer, what if she knows I'm gay, what if it tastes nasty, how long do I go for, how do I end it? I was DYING to kiss a guy but this was my chance to practise on someone I probably wasn't going to see ever again.

So, how'd it go, Riyadh?!

It was awful. Like, really awful. We must have looked like two gaping, suction-sealed mouth plungers. Our tongues were rotating like the inside of a tumble dryer so ferociously that I began to feel a nauseous. I opened my eyes once or twice during the ordeal to look around (presumably for help) while our face holes were still attached. She didn't appear to be stopping anytime soon. This girl had stamina. I began to feel saliva dribble from the corner of my mouth, but I wasn't sure if it was mine, hers or a combination of the two. I finally pulled away, said "Thank you" and proudly paraded back to "the lads" who cheered me on. Little did they know, I was crushing hard on them!

My first boy kiss happened a year later, outside a house party. He was standing against a tree and we were alone. I pondered to myself as I longingly looked at his beautiful face, "Can I do this? Is it wrong? Does he want it?" He was looking at me and I could tell we were probably thinking the same thing. He was one of the "straight guys" in my school, so I was taking a risk.

I took a deep breath and moved towards him, not knowing what the next few seconds were going to hold. Our lips touched and it was heaven on Earth. I can't tell you how incredible and overwhelming the rush was. All the burning lust that had been bubbling up in me for years had finally found an outlet in this one, gorgeous, guy. I was floating.

Our night ended up with us pressed against a neighbour's Nissan Micra exploring each other's bodies and our hidden desires. It was a night I'll never forget and one that brings a warm smile to my face whenever I think about it. What to know more about it? Turn to the My First Time chapter...

Although we are rarely in contact today, I'm happy I can still call this guy a friend of mine. I thank him for giving me the incredible gift of my first magical sexual experience with a guy.

KISSING – THINGS TO KNOW

Here's the big question when it comes to kissing: should you ask them before you lean in for a wet one?

Well, it all depends on the situation. Who is the person, how well do you know them, have you kissed them before, are you in a place where it's appropriate to land a smooch?

Say it's a boyfriend who you've kissed many times. It wouldn't be necessary to ask for a kiss in this situation. With my boyfriend, he knows that I want one with a simple longing look or I just jump right in and do it. But what if you're sitting beside someone you have the major hots for, and you can't quite initiate a kiss out of fear of rejection? We've all been there.

There's nothing wrong with asking for a kiss, but if the idea of doing that feels too awkward, try stating your desire outright by saying something like, "You know, I would really like to kiss you". Consent is always important when it comes to kissing or sex, and it works both ways. It's never okay to demand that someone kisses you, or to persuade them to against their will. Likewise, if someone tries to pressurize you into kissing them, say a firm "No" and walk away.

Happy smoochin'!

23

BEING SAFE IN PUBLIC

So you've come out, you're damn proud of your gayness, you wanna wear rainbow print from head to toe and kiss guys on the street while glitter falls from the sky and Troye Sivan tunes are blaring at full volume, right?! I hear ya, hun.

Please love and embrace everything about who you are, the way you speak, the way you want to dress and who you love, even if other people don't like it. It took me most of my adult life to realize that I didn't need to butch it up for fear of making others uncomfortable.

But the sad fact is, there are people out there who don't like us, so it's important to balance being authentically yourself with being safe.

Here are a few things we need to think about when expressing ourselves in public.

- Avoid places that are known as black spots for homophobia, particularly at night

- Be aware of events or situations that could pose a higher risk of danger like a football match, stag parties or groups of drunk lads on a train

- When you're walking alone, especially at night, take the well-lit route. Take your earphones out and stay around groups of people where possible

- If you're called a derogatory name, try to resist retaliating or provoking the person who said it. Leave the area quickly and quietly, then call the police. People shouting homophobic abuse at you is a hate crime, and it's important to report it

- If you want to kiss or hold hands with someone in public, then do it in places that are known as being safe for LGBT people. If possible, do it in an open public space

- If someone physically touches you, run away as fast as you can while calling out for help. Run towards light and other people

- If someone tries to steal from you, stay calm, give them what they want and call the police once they've gone

- If a person in a professional capacity (cab driver, sales assistant, waiter) is homophobic, then ask for their name and report the behaviour to their manager or company.

Homophobia can feel really personal, but it really isn't. Many of the people who flippantly shout homophobic comments don't really know the impact their words can have. It never feels nice when someone who knows nothing about you tries to humiliate you in public, but you and I know that we are SO much more than any insult. You are loved, you have a unique set of skills, interests, passions and dreams. And unlike the losers who sometimes shout at you, you're not aimlessly wandering the streets yelling nonsense at strangers!

You'll probably have to deal with homophobia a few times in your lifetime, but each time you're faced with it, it will hurt less and less. Because every time, you'll become stronger and more self-aware. You are beautiful and important. Remember that.

Don't try this at home

I was once kissing a guy after a night out on Waterloo Bridge in London. It was a gorgeous passionate moment – but as we were making out, a group of 16-year-old boys walked by, and one of them called out, "Ew! That's sick!"

I knew I shouldn't engage with him, but in the heat of the moment, I pulled away from the kiss and shouted at the boys to apologize. They started laughing, but I pointed at the boy who had commented on us, and in my best "angry mother" voice I demanded that he come back – and he did.

I said, "Do you realize the power of your words? You could cause a person to do something awful to themselves by saying something like that. I'm lucky. I don't care what you think about me. But for God's sake, think about it next time!"

To my surprise, the guy looked at me and said, "Sorry about that. I didn't mean it that way," and walked away. He'd tried to humiliate me, but he ended up way more embarrassed than I was.

I was lucky that time – but other times I've retaliated to homophobic abuse and made the situation worse. Just get out of there, and report it to the police. Staying safe is more important than making a point!

24

HEARTBREAK & BREAKUPS

If you're reading this through tears because your boyfriend just dumped you, I'm sorry! I've been there. Millions of us have been there. You WILL feel better and learn to love again (eventually). *virtual hug*

Why oh why do we put ourselves through such torture by laying our hearts on the line? Because love, true love, is always worth it. As clichéd as it sounds, every relationship, no matter if it's for one night, one year or one whole lifetime, teaches us priceless lessons about ourselves and how to treat others.

The crappy thing about a breakup is that it's almost like suffering a death, only weirder and perhaps worse (in your head) because the person is still alive, just out of reach and out of your life. Knowing that your former flame is still out there living, laughing and loving WITH-OUT you is bloody hard to take. But remember, you have the right to get out there and do all those things too.

Studies have shown that our bodies go through physical changes when we're suffering from heartbreak. It's something that needs to be taken seriously. If you're feeling heartbroken right now, your health and recovery must take priority. Even if those around you don't understand just how deeply you're hurting, know that I do and that there are small things you can do to alleviate the pain, even if it's just a little.

Try these in the early stages of heartbreak:

1. Talk to friends and family

2. Mute or unfollow your ex on social media – you need to not see him for a while

3. Seek professional help from a therapist

4. Get rid of all the songs, films and objects from your life that remind you of him

5. Challenge yourself to learn a new **enjoyable** and stress-free hobby you always wanted to try

6. Take time out from the non-essential stresses in your life like extra curricular activities – unless they help you take your mind off him

7. Get a haircut, a massage, a facial – treat yourself, hun!

8. Do all the great things you couldn't do when you were with him. Watch the films he didn't like, see the friends he didn't like hanging out with. Remind yourself why being single can be great.

Try these after some time has passed:

1. Get a new outfit, make yourself pretty and go to a party with friends – feel sexy again!

2. Try flirting or dating again to help you realize there ARE more great guys out there

3. Reach out to your ex for a friendly and calm "closure" call

4. Continue seeing a therapist if it feels right

Guys can be a blessing and a curse, but take this from someone who has been devastated by heartbreak twice and is now madly, deeply in love: it is worth it in the end.

Look after yourself and be gentle with every heart you manage to capture. His heart is just as delicate as your own!

AJ from Columbus wrote to me after his breakup:

"I was dating this guy for just over a year and then out of nowhere he dropped the "I'm not feeling this anymore" bomb. It felt like a dagger to my soul. The worst thing? He did it while we were staying at his parents' house for his mother's birthday.

For the next three days I had to sit and ponder our relationship and if it had ever meant anything to him while fighting back tears and singing 'Happy birthday' to the woman I'd fully believed was going to be my mother-in-law. I didn't sleep a wink and thought that by the time we returned home he would have changed his mind. Surprise! He didn't.

They say it takes about half the length of the relationship to get over it. That would mean about 6 months for me. Well, 9 months on I am still thinking about it and I occasionally get upset, but I am stronger and happier now. I didn't realize it at the time, but it was a toxic relationship. Being out of it has helped me so much.

I now put myself first, I give my friends and family the time they deserve, I've started seeing a therapist who has saved me in more ways than one and my career is doing great. I've started dating again too. This time I'm so much more aware of the mind games my ex used to put me through, so I can make sure history doesn't repeat itself. Okay, the breakup was nasty, but it was a blessing in disguise."

Jin Yong

Jin Yong is an award-winning artist. He was born in China, but he's currently based in Ireland.

If I could give my younger self one piece of advice, it would be "Accept who you are." I'm Korean, but I was born and raised in China, and I moved to Ireland on my own when I was 21. I was also a gay boy, growing up in a Christian family. I have faced many struggles in my life, but being gay was the hardest of all. I've known I was gay since I had a dream about a boy in my class when I was 9 years old. I prayed to God to cure me every single day until I was 30. God answered hundreds if not thousands of my prayers, but the one prayer he didn't answer was to change me into a straight man. In my thirties, I finally realized that God made me the way I am and I found inner peace. Now I can live a free, happy life.

I call my self "EFIL", because I Easily Fall In Love. I fancied so many boys as a kid and a teenager, but because I was hiding my identity, I only had my first relationship when I was 23. I wasted all those beautiful years. My advice to young gay guys is to express your feelings. It's okay to be rejected because you'll find beautiful souls everywhere when you have the courage to face people with love and hope.

All
about
bodies.

If you were born with a penis, you can expect some of these delights to occur in the process of growing up:

Your mood will fluctuate – you'll be happy one minute, furious seconds later.

Your skin may break out in spots and become oily.

Hair might grow on other parts of your body, too – your armpits, belly, chest, and your face.

Your voice may deepen.

You'll sweat more, and you'll notice that you smell more too.

Pubic hair starts to grow.

Your penis will grow larger.

You may have a growth spurt.

Your balls start to produce semen.

Your balls will grow larger and hang lower.

Your scrotum (ball sack) will get darker.

25

WHAT'S GOING ON WITH MY BODY?! (PUBERTY, THAT'S WHAT)

HAIRY BALLS!!

Yeah, I knew that'd get your attention. And to be honest, a hairy ball sack is gonna to be the least of your worries, buddy. Strap in and let's go for a whirl through the peculiar perils of puberty. It ain't all bad, but seeing your body change into something new, smelly and prickly can be a bit scary. Just remember, whatever happens, it's probably totally normal. I'll run through what to expect, why your body changes and what you should do about it (usually nothing). I've written this chapter based on my experience as a cis boy who grew up to be a cis man, so it'll be most relevant to people with penises. Puberty will be different for people with vulvas, but some of this advice will apply to everyone.

Unfortunately, puberty isn't like a reliable takeaway that you know will arrive an hour after you've placed the order. It's as if someone else (Mother Nature) has placed your puberty order for you, and they've not told you what they've selected from the menu. Plus everything will arrive at random times, when you least expect (or want) them.

Cis boys go through puberty slightly later than cis girls. As girls start to throw monthly period parties, boys are only just discovering the first curly pubes growing out of the base of their willies. "YES! I'm a man" you may exclaim. But remember, everybody is different and some bodies take longer to start puberty than others. So don't worry if your friends seem to be ahead of you.

When will it happen?

When you're going through puberty, your body is a bit like a caterpillar, getting ready to come out of a cocoon as a butterfly. The process takes time. It's slow, full of surprises and happens in stages, but it's so worth it.

Most cis boys experience the changes between the ages of 12 and 16 years old. For me and some of my friends, it was a little later. So get used to being a temperamental, horny and emotional ball of hormones – puberty usually lasts about four years! Although puberty is usually over by the time you're 18, even now, aged 27, I'm still noticing changes in my voice, skin and facial hair. Now I can finally grow a (patchy) moustache!

Your body is constantly changing and evolving. It used to annoy and even upset me that once I became comfortable with my body the way it was, it would go and change AGAIN. I've now learned to enjoy the morphing of my body and find it endlessly entertaining. It's like watching a Pokemon evolve. For example, nose hair. WTF?! I thought that was for granddads. Apparently not! I'm trimming those bad boys every two weeks now. Sexy.

Take care of yourself

With the colossal shifts in your body and life that come with puberty, things can feel out of control. You may feel a new wave of emotions, anxieties and stresses that you didn't have to deal with before. Once you were interested in playing rounders and watching cartoons with your friends, and now your attention is shifting to your future goals, your burning attraction to that gorgeous guy in your class and the fear of not being "good enough" at school. But you are doing just fine. All these feelings are normal and to be expected. Your body was already growing fast as a kid but now it's in turbo-mode and you're not in the driving seat.

Hold on tight, make sure you ask for directions, pull over and take a break to talk to someone if you need to and be confident that you'll reach your destination, no matter how bumpy and hormonal the road is.

What if people don't get it?

It's been a long, long time since your parents, teachers and the other adults in your life went through what you're going through. So don't take it personally if they don't seem to understand your frustrations. I remember having these out-of-the blue RAGE attacks. Something tiny would happen – a bus might drive past me without stopping – and instead of being disappointed and annoyed at having to wait for the next one, I would scream, swear and wave my hands about like a lunatic.

I didn't know it then, but I know it now: my mind was stuck in a cloud of potent pubescent chemicals. If you notice yourself swinging from joy to rage to sadness to anxiety to numbness, then give yourself a break. Acknowledge that it's not your fault – your body and mind are in flux. Take a seat, have a breather and talk to someone like a school counsellor about the way you're feeling. That's what they're there for.

Enjoy this rollercoaster ride. You will never change this drastically and this fast at any other point in your life. Instead of fearing the changes, look forward to them and allow yourself to get excited every time one pops up... apart from an erection in maths class. Nobody wants that.

26

AWKWARD BONERS

Boners. The word
alone makes you want
to giggle, doesn't it?

It sounds silly and childish, and when you say it, you might feel like you've said something naughty. But you haven't! Boners exist, and we can talk about them as much as we want to. Some of my teachers disagreed with my open and regular penis chat, but hey, I'm an adult now, so... BONERS BONERS BONERS!

Boners are life's biggest contradiction. They bring us sheer joy one minute and utter embarrassment the next. It all comes down to timing and who's around when you get one.

We may laugh at erections, or feel ashamed when they surprise us, but let's face it: none of us would exist if it weren't for the mighty boner! So a little respect wouldn't go amiss.

Awkward boners can pop up for all sorts of reasons and it's not always because we're turned on. Baby boys can have boners right through childhood – some foetuses even get them in the womb – and most men have around five boners each night while they're sleep. Erections are natural, yes, but they take on a life of their own once we reach puberty! When you go through puberty, more testosterone starts charging around your body and the slightest vibration or sensual thought can make the pal who lives in your trousers go from tired earthworm to proud flagpole.

> **We may laugh at erections, or feel ashamed when they surprise us, but let's face it: none of us would exist if it weren't for the mighty boner!**

So, you're in a place where you REALLY do not want a boner and then, BAM! There he is. Here's how to minimize your pointed peen:

Hide it

When your ruler is ridged, the worst thing you can do is to try and bend it downwards. It will make the situation all the more obvious, it'll hurt like hell and you could inadvertently injure yourself. Without putting your hands down your pants, try to wriggle your lower half and manoeuvre your penis so he's facing upwards and pressed flat onto your stomach. Cover your trousers with your hands to hide what you're doing. You may be able to hold him in place with your trouser waistband or belt while pulling a jumper or t-shirt over the area until he gets tired and the crisis is averted.

Think it away

Sometime you get a boner because of a thought that got you excited. Sometimes you get them for no reason at all. No matter what triggered the southward rush of blood, there is no denying the strong connection between your two most treasured body parts: your brain and penis. Make sure you have a go-to thought that will help you go floppy in a moment of panic. It goes without saying, the less sexy the image or thought, the better. Some friends of mine think of a boring sports match or a pile of dog poo, or they try to solve a difficult sum. Personally, I always used to think about dead bodies. I know, I'm an odd soul. Why did you buy my book?! I'm hanging my head in shame – but at least I don't have an awks boner!

Location, location, location

Every day, on the bus home from school, I would try to avoid the back row of seats. It was near the engine, which made the seats really warm, the motor below made the whole area vibrate, and as the bus drove along, over ramps and potholes, the back of the vehicle bounced rhythmically up and down. As you can imagine, the back of the bus was a boner breeding ground and an absolute nightmare for 15-year-old Riyadh. I can't tell you the number of times I had to miss my stop and walk a half hour back on myself because it took me ten stops to get my lad down. In this kind of situation, try to find a spot on the bus, car, train, tram or cable car that is less likely to wake up your one-eyed trouser snake. Try standing or move to the front of the vehicle. Do whatever you have to do!

The art of distraction

One day in class, our teacher was making us stand up one by one and point to a specific country on a world map on the other side of the room. As the teacher moved from one pupil to the next, I could see my friend Nathan begin to blush. Soon he was sweaty and wide-eyed, and he had look of sheer panic on his face. I had no idea what was wrong with him until I heard the teacher say, "Nathan, can you please get up and show us where Cyprus is on the map, please." He stood up, and thirty or so students all got an eyeful of poor Nathan's situation. That's the type of stuff that sticks with you for life!

If you find yourself in Nathan's position, DEFLECT DEFLECT DEFLECT! Tell the teacher you're not feeling well and need to put your head down for a second. Pretend you have no idea where the hell

Cyprus is and ponder on it until Mr Willyman has gone down. Ask the teacher to come back to you a little later. Pretend you've suddenly lost the ability to see and hear. Do whatever it takes.

Accept it

Even with all these tools (lol) of the trade, you may still find yourself in a situation where the world can see that you're stashing a flesh pistol in your pants. In this case, I say stand tall, stand proud and own it. "Yeah, it's a boner, sometimes I get them, are you done looking now?"

Awkward boners are really nothing to be ashamed of. Getting occasional hard-ons is your body's way of telling you that it's in fine working order. There may come a day later in life when you find it hard to get it up, so enjoy how spritely he is right now!

27

WET DREAMS

Just when you thought the body changes, mood swings, awkward boners and endless pimples that come with puberty were enough, along come the sticky surprises lovingly known as wet dreams. Grab the wet wipes because we're about to jump into some seriously messy territory!

As people with penises go through puberty, the reproductive organs – including the prostate gland (up your bum) and balls (you know where they are) – begin to produce semen. My mate Darren used to scare the bejesus out of me by telling me semen would come flying out of the tip of my penis without warning, that it'd be green and would sting like hell. I used to sit, looking at my little man down below, waiting for the semen to appear like the exorcist, spewing green vomit across the bed-

When your body has extra semen it wants to get rid of, and your mind is running wild thinking of hot guys while you're in deep sleep, you might have a wet dream.

room. But luckily, it turns out Darren was either a compulsive liar or horrendously misinformed, because semen is nothing like that at all.

Semen, or cum, is what we all started life as! Well, the combination of sperm and your mother's egg. Semen is a mixture of sperm and the fluid they swim in, which is full of minerals and sugars to give the little swimmers energy for their epic trek to fertilize an egg … or their journey into a tissue or a crusty sock. Yes, I'm looking at you.

When your body has extra semen it wants to get rid of, and your mind is running wild thinking of hot guys while you're in deep sleep, you might have a wet dream. This is an involuntary ejaculation of semen that usually leaves you with a nasty mess to clean up in the morning. Some people have loads of wet dreams a month. Others never have them at all. I never had a wet dream in my early teens – to be honest,

I NEVER HAD A WET DREAM IN MY EARLY TEENS – TO BE HONEST, I FELT LIKE I WAS MISSING OUT ON ALL THE SPERMY ACTION!

I felt like I was missing out on all the spermy action! Thinking back now, it's clear to me why I never had one in the early days: I was already touching myself and ejaculating so much that there wasn't much left to squirt out during my randy sleepy fantasies.

My first and only wet dream came (lol) after I had spent a week in a tent with a close girlfriend of mine at a Spanish music festival. I was horny as hell after seeing hundreds of gorgeous Spanish jocks walking around topless. I couldn't relieve myself, because I was glued to my camping companion 24/7, and by the end of the week I was ready to explode.

When I got back to my own bedroom, I planned to blow a load, but I was so knackered that I passed out. The next morning, I woke to a destroyed bed. Initially I thought I had wet myself, but then I felt the stickiness and smelt that bleachy smell you'll soon learn to know well. I laughed and then felt like I'd wasted it all on a dream I couldn't remember!

If you have a wet dream, remember it's a normal, natural process and it just means that your mind and body are communicating and doing what they're supposed to do. Your parents shouldn't judge you for having wet dreams – we're all young once, and they'll know it's totally normal – but obviously it's a bit of an embarrassing thing to talk to them about!

Want to keep your nighttime leakage private? Try these tips:

- If the mess has reached your sheets, change the bed clothes while your parents are asleep or out of the house (YouTube can show you how). Throw the dirty sheets in the washing machine. Your parents will think you're a legend for changing your bed without being forced to!

- Soak your dirty underwear or pyjamas in the bathroom sink with warm water and shower gel. Rinse them out and hang them somewhere discreet to dry, and no one will be any the wiser.

28

PRE-CUM

Sex is a complex business, but the human body has some clever ways of making things run more smoothly. One of these is a wondrous substance known as pre-cum.

Pre-cum is exactly what the name suggests: a fluid that appears before you cum. It's a clear liquid, because it's made up of semen, but without any sperm – it's sperm that gives semen the cloudy white colour you see when you ejaculate. Light bulb moment, eh?!

Pre-cum acts as a natural lubricant to help with penetrative sex, although it's important to remember that you should always use a condom and water-based lubricant if you're having sex – that way you'll protect yourself and your partner from a whole host of nasty sexually transmitted infections. See the chapter on STIs for more information on how to protect yourself and what symptoms to look out for. Sorry to scare you, but this stuff is important.

If you're getting intimate with a dude and he starts gushing pre-cum, don't be startled... It means he is proper turned on and into you. BOOM!

Although pre-cum generally doesn't contain sperm, it is still possible to get a female partner pregnant if you have a sexual encounter and don't wear a condom. Remember, it just takes a single sperm to fertilize an egg, so it's always better to play it safe if you do decide to try out sexy time with ladies.

I've seen lots of erect penises, including my own, and speaking from experience, you might not get any pre-cum at all, or you might have so much that you'd need a couple of tissues to mop it up. If you're getting intimate with a dude and he starts gushing pre-cum, don't be startled. If anything, see it as a compliment. It means he is proper turned on and into you. Boom!

It's easy to wash pre-cum (and semen) from your clothes, so don't panic if your favourite black boxer briefs look like a slug has been squashed in them after a make-out session with your crush. A quick spin in the washing machine will have them good as new.

PSA

Never confuse pre-cum – a clear, odourless fluid that comes out of your penis when you're aroused – with other fluids. If you get a yellow or green discharge with an unpleasant smell, this could be a sign of an infection such as chlamydia or gonorrhoea.

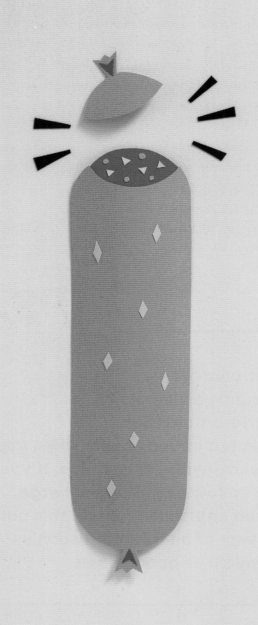

29

CIRCUMCISION

"Hey dude, r u cut or uncut?"

This is the kind of dating/hookup app message guys see quite often. It's a question that makes you question your body and your attractiveness, and it's horrible – someone's judging you before they've even met you, based on something you have absolutely no control over.

When I was about two weeks old my parents made the decision to have me circumcised for cultural reasons. The description of the process may make your eyes water, but I'm going to tell you about it anyway. A doctor surgically removed the protective skin around the sensitive head of my penis by placing a small, pointed piece of metal under the foreskin, rolling it side to side and breaking the membrane attaching it to the glands before cutting it off with a scalpel. He then stitched the wound on the shaft of my penis shut. The wound had to be cleaned daily with an iodine solution. Not the most pleasant experience for a newborn baby, is it?

Infant male circumcision is an ancient tradition that has been carried out all over the world for centuries, particularly in Muslim and Jewish communities. In some cultures, children are circumcised for religious reasons. Some believe that circumcised penises are cleaner, and that it reduces the spread of disease. Some people need to be circumcised for medical reasons – because their foreskin doesn't retract properly, or it gets infected. 71% of men in the US are circumcised, but only 21% of men in the UK – and just 1% in Ireland.

Circumcision can reduce the risk of contracting HIV from a woman during sex, and circumcised men are less likely to get urinary tract infections. But most of the time circumcision isn't medically necessary, and once the foreskin is removed, there's no way to bring it back. Tens of thousands of vital nerve endings that give sexual pleasure are severed, and over time, the sensitivity of the penis head is reduced by the friction it's exposed to from clothing, heat and cold, now that it doesn't have the foreskin to protect it. Grim but true.

When I first read up about this procedure, which was carried out on me without my consent, I was horrified and very upset. It led to heated arguments in my house which went a little like this:

Me: Why did you allow someone to do this to me as a baby?

Mom/ Dad: It was for your own good!

Me: I have been mutilated and altered for life!

Mom/Dad: Don't be silly! Circumcised penises look nicer than uncut penises, and they're way cleaner.

Me: Who the hell are you to judge the "beauty" of a person's genitals? And by the way, I shower every day, so having or not having a foreskin isn't going to change my cleanliness.

The arguments went on for a couple of years until my parents eventually apologized and agreed that they should have waited till I was old enough to make the life-altering decision to be circumcised myself. It took me a long time to love my penis again, and accepting that I can't change it back to its natural state will be a lifelong process. For years I was anxious about how my penis looked, because I was born in a country where very few boys are circumcised. Whenever I dropped my pants in the bedroom, the guy would say, "Oh, you're cut!" Bit of a boner killer for me, even if they were into it.

Because I'm circumcised, I used to find it quite hard to cum during sex, or need quite intense friction to reach orgasm. I still need more friction than someone who is uncut, but now that I've found a partner who I feel 100% comfortable with, I have been able to reach climax naturally. It feels amazing.

Andy from Newcastle had his foreskin removed when he was 26 years old, for medical reasons:

"I was terrified about the long-term affect being circumcised would have on my very active mid-twenties sex life. I was also petrified about the pain. For a while, I considered living with my stuck foreskin, but after a couple of dudes who I had one-night stands with commented on it, I decided to have the chop.

I'm not going to lie, the pain was like nothing I've felt before, and I've had several tattoos. But after about a month, I looked down and I was happy that I could see my head again – he had been hidden away for two years. At first my newly freed dick was super-sensitive – I was very aware of it rubbing against by boxers when I walked – but after a while I got used to it. My sex life is pretty much the same as before, and a few guys actually say they prefer my circumcised dick. A win for me, I guess.'

If you're circumcised and anxious about it, like I was, there's support out there. On the flip side, you may like being circumcised and happy that your parents made the decision for you while you were young enough to not remember it! No matter what, never judge someone on the size, appearance or performance of their penis. A throwaway comment could stick with someone for years and affect their confidence in and out of the bedroom. Be kind and love all penises. Simple!

BODY IMAGE

In a world where we are bombarded with images of Insta-models and dudes on magazine covers with washboard abs and bulbous biceps, it's no surprise that many of us look at ourselves and play a dangerously destructive game of spot-the-difference.

It's a game that leaves us thinking that the polished Adonis we see online is the only acceptable body shape – that all other body types are not only unattractive, but most devastatingly, unlovable.

Hey, look, I'll be the first to put my hand up and admit that looking at those fine physiques is a treat. But that doesn't mean you have to look like them. Do you know how many hours those guys put into looking like that?! You've gotta be able to **love yourself as you are right now.**

I spent most of my teens and twenties with body confidence issues. When I had no body hair I wished I had it, then when I had it I wished I didn't. I wanted to be muscular but I didn't have the interest or motivation to work out. I then put on a little weight (as you do when an ever-changing cocktail of hormones starts racing through your body) and I hated it, so I started starving my self until I almost collapsed. I really wish I had been okay with the way I looked in the moment, and that I had been chill with the inevitable changes that were going to take place over the years.

One day in my mid-twenties, as I was lying in bed on a Sunday morning with my ex-boyfriend, he casually said, "I wish you were more toned." It was one of many throw-away comments he made about my body that I convinced myself at the time were innocent or even encouraging. Before long, our relationship was over, but his words stuck with me and began to fester.

For about three years after that, I felt shame and anxiety about my body. It wasn't incapacitating by any means, but when I was getting naked in front of a new partner I would often resort to dim lighting or darkness, or wearing my boxer briefs high up my waist to soften or cinch my tummy area. Apparently loads of guys do this when they're feeling insecure!

But over the last 18 months I've decided to reclaim my sexuality, my confidence and my body in all of its imperfect glory. Here are seven practical tools I've used to boost my body confidence and start loving the skin I'm in. I really hope they work for you too.

1 Touch yourself and let him touch you

Like any anxiety, one of the surest ways of overcoming negative feelings about your body is to face them head on. I hated my "pooch", that small lump of insulation around my tummy. I recently asked a guy I was dating to tell me what he thought of it. I was surprised to hear he loved it. While in bed, I asked him to place his hand on it and to stop avoiding the area as I had previously asked him to do. Breaking that wall seemed insignificant to him but it was HUGE to me. I could feel part of my insecurity falling away instantly.

2 Make positive your default

Ask your friends and family to tell you specific things they like about your body. This could be anything from your eyes to the way you laugh or your strong jawline. Focus on celebrating these areas instead of letting your confidence be affected by a stretch mark, muffin top or flabby booty. Hearing people you trust tell you what they love about you can shift your mindset for the better.

3 Call it out

It's an unfortunate truth that some people in the gay male community enjoy passing judgment on other people's appearances for fun. They often justify it by saying things like, "What they can't hear won't hurt them." But even though it might be subconscious, this behavior creates pressure to conform to unrealistic body standards, and it leaves us all feeling judged. Laughing at body-shaming comments validates them and makes the problem worse. If you hear anyone shaming a lover, a friend, a passerby or someone they've seen online, politely ask them to stop.

4 Weed out shame producers

Look deep into your life – not just at your lovers, friends and family but also at the people you follow on social media. Ask yourself, "Where does my body shame come from?" You might remember a throwaway comment from a work colleague or an ex who pressured you to eat a certain way, but you might also be affected by the unhealthy number of ripped guys you follow on Instagram. Be proactive in removing these people and influences from your life. Cut out people who treat you badly in real life, and curate your social media feeds so that they only feature content that makes you feel good about yourself. You deserve to be surrounded by people who love and appreciate you just the way you are.

 ## 5 Stop chasing THAT guy

When you're dating someone or just chatting on an app, look out for warning signs. If the guy you like mentions the gym every second sentence, asks for body pics too soon, or over-fetishizes a "perfect" body type, then cut your losses and move on to someone who is looking for everything else you have to offer! He may be hot and physically your type, but if he's going to make you feel empty and unattractive then don't waste your precious emotional energy and time on him.

 ## 6 Make one small change

You don't need to become a gym bunny or a fitness model, but cutting out that one sugary drink a day, trying to eat a little healthier or being more active once or twice a week will boost your endorphins and energy levels and do wonders for your mental clarity. Exercise is amazing for your mental health and it can help you feel more motivated in all areas of your life. Plus you might see some positive physical changes, which in turn will boost your body confidence.

7 Ask for help

If you're lacking body confidence, try talking to someone you trust about it. This will take the problem out of your head, and you can start working on overcoming the problem. You could start by telling a friend or someone in your family, or you might feel better talking to a therapist. I went to see a counsellor to talk about my

Asking for help can be daunting and may make you feel even more vulnerable, but trust me, it's worth it.

chronic anxiety, and it quite literally changed my life. Before I sought professional help, I had recurring panic attacks that left me unable to function at work, drive my car safely or form friendships. Asking for help can be daunting and may make you feel even more vulnerable, but trust me, it's worth it. As clichéd as it sounds, a problem shared definitely is a problem halved. By talking through your body insecurities, you will probably discover that the most outwardly confident people in your life also suffer with similar body-image issues to you. It all comes down to this: your body does not, and should not, define you. It's just a vessel that you live in. It will change over and over again throughout your life and there is nothing you can do about that. Be kind to it, look after it, keep it nourished and active, but accept it just the way it is now – not the way you want it to be in the future. People won't remember you for the way your body looks. Work on loving yourself for your personality, talents, passions and your relationships with other people. These will last the test of time and bring you true, authentic happiness.

MATTHEW TODD

Matthew Todd is a writer and the former editor of *Attitude* magazine. His book *Straight Jacket* is out now.

Growing gay in a hostile world really took its toll on me. For a long time, I felt less than other people, so I compensated by striving to be better than everyone. I'd tell my 16-year-old self that living your best life isn't about being "fabulous", it's about healing the damage done to your self esteem by society's gay shame. For me, it was about learning to ignore the voice in my head that tells me I'm not good enough, so that I'm now able to be a good friend, a good son, a good brother, a good uncle, and potentially a good partner, but most importantly, I have the ability to really like, love and value myself.

Let's talk about sex.

31

PUSH YOUR OWN BUTTONS

Humans have masturbated since the dawn of time. It is TOTALLY NATURAL and many young boys and girls start playing with their privates from as young as five or six! It's only when we reach puberty that the sexual element really comes alive.

When I was thirteen, I gave myself my first hand job. Well, it was more of an arm job – I was naked and I got an unexplained erection while I was lying in bed. (You know what it's like, lads – he pops up to say hi even when you haven't asked for it!) I was pondering the homework I hadn't done and what ridiculous excuse I was going to tell my Maths teacher in the morning when I reached down to pull the covers over my body. I accidentally rubbed my forearm against the hard head of my penis and WOW. Okay, I thought, let's do that again, shall we? HOLY MOTHER OF GOD. What was this feeling? Why was it so nice? Why hadn't I been told about this trick before? I began to push my hairless forearm back and forth over my dick like I was playing a violin. It felt wonderful – but eventually I got tired and passed out without cumming. I might have been too young to ejaculate, anyway.

From that day on, my poor penis hasn't been left alone for more

than a few hours at a time. Masturbating is totally harmless – though your junk can get a bit sore if you don't leave it alone. But sometimes it can get addictive. If you feel worried about how much you masturbate, it might be a good idea to talk to someone about it – a family member you can be open with, or a doctor. There is no shame in asking for help.

If you masturbate a lot, you might find that it's hard to come unless you do it in a certain way – a way that no other person can replicate. This might mean you find it hard to come with someone else. To overcome this, try to mix things up a bit. If you're used to jerking with your right hand then swap it to the left, loosen your grip, try with or without lube, slow down the pace, tease your penis for longer and enjoy a slower, drawn out session. Sexual pleasure of any kind shouldn't be rushed!

JACKING OFF

One of nature's utterly wondrous gifts.

- It's free
- It feels amazing
- It releases hormones that naturally suppress pain
- You learn how you like to be touched – and what you don't like.
- It can help combat insomnia
- You become more connected to your body, less afraid of it and more educated about how it works
- It relieves stress
- It's healthy

32

P-O-R-N

It was a long weekend, and my parents were away.

I went through their wardrobe to find a spare belt because I had lost mine (again). As I rifled through layer after layer of my mother and father's formal wear, I came across a neat pile of DVDs in clear plastic sleeves. There were pictures of naked men and women on the front. I grabbed one and took it straight to the living room. Was this one of those porno things the lads in school were so obsessed with?

I drew the blinds, locked the doors and started watching the DVD. At first, I was horrified: a man and woman were roughly pounding each other, screaming and saying things like, "Ooh yeah, give it to me." Why would anyone want to do this awful sex thing? It looked barbaric! But before long, I began to enjoy it. The awful acting obviously appealed to my dramatic side. I got bored of that DVD and I wanted new material, so I searched Google for "sexy naked hunk" (so tame!). I waited for what felt like a lifetime (this was dial-up internet) as a single image slowly loaded onto the screen, starting with his head and buffering down his body like a pixel-by-pixel strip tease, until I realized that the dude was wearing underwear and my half-hour wait had been for nothing. DAMMIT!

My early experiences of porn were certainly... memorable.

There are good things about porn. And believe it or not, it isn't just a way to make yourself feel horny. Porn can normalize LGBT+ sex –

sex that is rarely seen or celebrated in mainstream film and TV. This allows queer people to feel recognized and shows that queer sex is just as natural and beautiful as heterosexual sex. Think of how many loved-up straight couples you see on the street, on billboards, on TV and on social media. It's not that I don't want to see this kind of love – all love is bloody brilliant – but when I was young, gay porn felt like a balancing force in a world that revolved around straight couples.

But there are lots of bad things about porn, too. Now that it's so easy to access porn over the internet, increasing numbers of children and teenagers are being exposed to it. Over 50% of 11-16 year olds have seen some form of explicit material online. Many young people learn about sex by watching porn, and that isn't healthy. Because porn isn't realistic, or real – it's a show. The actors have been chosen for what they look like – they're thin or curvy or muscley, with huge penises and breasts. Most people don't look like that in IRL. Remember that almost all of the stuff you find online, including the amateur videos filmed on a dodgy camera propped up against an air conditioning unit, all include an element of performance. And young people sometimes feel as though they should match the noises, the aggression, the positions and the stamina of the performers, even though it might not feel natural to them.

It's so important to have sex in a way that makes you feel good – and that makes your partner feel good, too. The best way to make sure that's happening is to get their consent, and to communicate with each other about what's going on – and you don't often see consent-seeking and communication in porn. Plus people in porn hardly ever wear condoms... whereas you should ALWAYS use a condom during sex!

It's also possible to become desensitized by watching too much porn. We are sexual beings, so we're hardwired to get turned on when we see something sexy. Our eyes go wide, our hearts beat faster, and our penises do that thing they do. These changes are triggered by a series of chemical reactions in our brains. Neat, right?! But when you see images and videos of hot naked men every day for weeks, your brain will get used to it and soon it won't be enough to give you the hit of endorphins and adrenaline you're looking for. You'll start to crave more and more graphic porn to get the high you need. Porn can be addictive, just like drugs or alcohol.

Graphic porn comes in many forms – group sex, rough sex, role play – the list goes on. We all have certain things we find sexy. It can be fun trying new things to see what does it for you. But if you notice that you're starting to need more and more intense or out-there porn to get a buzz, it's worth considering a porn detox. In a world where porn is available at your fingertips, real-life sex can actually seem like a chore to some guys, and some even develop erectile dysfunction. This is usually reversed when they stop over-consuming porn.

There are also ethical questions around porn. When you're watching mainstream porn, it's hard to tell whether the people involved have to consented to everything they're doing, or whether they are being exploited. There are companies that make "ethical" or "free-trade" porn, where the performers are treated with respect and have consented in advance to everything that happens in a scene – but if you're watching free porn online, you can't be sure that's the case.

My good friend Shane Jenek, aka Courtney Act, told me that he had recently discovered the damaging affects of porn. Now instead of watching porn, he relies on the memories of his past sexual encounters to get him off. It's a process I've tried myself, and after a mere week of abstaining from digital ding-dongs, the memory of an IRL sexual experience is SO SO much better. The best part? You don't need an

SEXUAL CONSENT

Sex is great – but only when you're old enough and everyone involved is up for it. So let's talk about consent. Sure, the word might sound a bit serious and clinical, but it's a vital part of sex.

Remember: Sexual consent is yours to give, yours to take back at any moment, and yours to outright refuse.

This is an area that confuses a lot of people. How do I get consent? How do I give consent? What if I change my mind? Am I legally able to give consent? What does it mean?

Ideas about sexual consent has changed A LOT over time. When our parents were growing up, people assumed someone had consented to sex if they hadn't explicitly said "no" to a sexual advance. Now things

are all about positive affirmation. Before you have sex, everyone involved should give an enthusiastic **"yes"**, otherwise you should presume consent has not been given.

"What's an enthusiastic yes?"

It's self-explanatory, really. Not all "yesses" are the same. If a person is being coerced or pressured to say yes, then this does not count as consent. Consent is when someone says yes out of their own **free will**, without anyone influencing them or forcing them to. Read their body language, their tone of voice, the way they're looking at you. If they've said yes verbally but they seem fearful, worried or unsure, take a step back. It has to be enthusiastic to count as consent. It's important to point out that a person can be nervous about having sex and still consent. Maybe it's their first time or maybe they really fancy you and feel worried about messing up! It's all about what THEY want in that moment. Make sure THEY make the decision on their own.

There are situations where someone may say an enthusiastic yes, but it still doesn't count as consent. Turn the page to find out why...

When a person can't consent:

- If they're under the age of consent
- If they're drunk or have taken drugs
- If they're asleep or unconscious
- If they've been kidnapped or held against their will
- If they have been threatened into saying yes

But what should I say?

Words and phrases you could use to give consent or refuse consent in different situations:

You want to consent to one sexual act but not to another.

"I want to have oral sex but I don't want to have anal sex."

You've consented to a sexual act , but you change your mind before or during the event

"I don't want to do this anymore. Please stop." You can withdrawn your consent at any time. The sexual activity must stop right away.

Someone has made a sexual advance and asked you to have sex with them but you don't want to

"I don't want to have sex." Simple but effective!

No lifetime pass

Just because you've given someone consent once or several times in the past, that doesn't mean they have an automatic right to have sex with you whenever they want to. Sexual consent is not a sex voucher valid for a lifetime. It is a time-sensitive pass only valid in the present and always determined by those granting it.

Be vigilant of how a person is feeling

Remember, even though your sexual partner may have uttered the words "Yes, I consent", there's still a chance that they might have changed their mind and want to stop. They could be too worried, embarrassed or awkward to say it out loud. Look out for some key cues: if they are closed off, reserved or seem to be moving their body away from you, then stop and politely and calmly ask if they want to continue. Likewise, if they aren't moving, or if they're trembling then check in on them to see if they're still enjoying what's going on.

I wish that I'd had the confidence to say "No, I don't want to do this" when I was first exploring my sexuality. Instead, I found myself in situations where I felt obliged to carry on with a sexual activity even though my heart was telling me to stop. There is no shame in saying no and it does not make you boring or prudish. It in fact makes you a strong and independent young person, in control of your body and how others get to interact with it.

(34)

WHAT COUNTS AS SEX?

This is the big one!

When I was younger, the word alone would send me into a tizzy – it was a dirty, filthy, flirty thing that I didn't totally understand yet. I knew I was a product of my parents having sex (vom) but how the hell did you do it and how was I supposed to feel about it?

Fast forward a few years. I've gone through puberty and things have changed. Now I certainly know how I feel about sex. It's great!

Sex is an extremely personal expression of passion, connection, lust and love. Sometimes just a couple of those elements are present when you're doing it, and other (amazing) times you experience all four.

What if I don't want to have sex?

Not wanting to have sex is completely normal. Maybe you don't feel ready yet. Or maybe you don't experience sexual attraction to anyone. That could mean that you're asexual. Again, you're totally normal, and you shouldn't do anything you don't want to do. People feel ready for sex at different times, and some people never want to do. Try not to worry about what your friends are doing. Just make sure you're doing what feels right to you.

Different kinds of sex

There are endless ways to have sex. If you think you're having sex then you probably are having sex. Sex varies from person to person and situation to situation. We're brought up in a heteronormative world where sex between a man and woman, when a penis enters a vagina, is seen as the only kind of "real" sex. But that's nonsense. People assume that all gay men have anal sex, but that's not true either. Plenty of gay guys enjoy great sex lives even though they never have penetrative sex. Here are just some of the many, many ways you can enjoy sex.

Masturbation

When you touch yourself, you find out what you enjoy and how you like to be touched. It's not bad for you – in fact, it's good for you! But it's your choice whether you do it or not.

Mutual masturbation

When you touch the sensitive parts of your partner's body.

Non-penetrative sex

Any kind of sex that doesn't involve penetration.

Penetrative sex

Penetrative sex is when you penetrate your partner's anus or mouth (or vagina) with your penis, your finger or something else, like a dildo or sex toy. Oral, anal and vaginal sex all count as penetrative sex.

Oral sex

Using your mouth to stimulate your partner's genital area. If you hear people talking about "giving head" or "going down" on someone, this is what they're talking about. Oral sex totally counts as sex, and it's very easy to pass on STIs by having oral sex, so always use a condom. Here are some of the different kinds of oral sex:

- Analingus, also known as rimming. This is when someone stimulates their partner's anus using their mouth or tongue.

- Cunnilingus – when someone uses their mouth to stimulate their partner's vagina and/or clitoris.

- Fellatio, otherwise known as a blowjob. This is when someone uses their mouth or tongue to stimulate their partner's penis

Sex can be a mix of all the above, but licking, kissing, biting and touching each other's bodies also counts. What I've learned from my friends across the queer spectrum is that sex is whatever you make it. There are no rules about what counts or doesn't count. So, when you're ready, sex is yours to explore, discover and play with.

Staying safe

What ever kind of sex you have, remember to use protection. Even if you're not having penetrative sex, you can still catch a sexually transmitted infection, so ALWAYS USE A CONDOM!

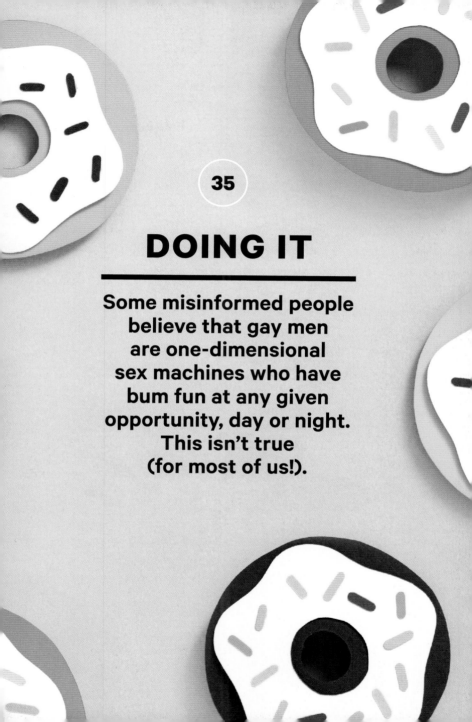

35

DOING IT

Some misinformed people
believe that gay men
are one-dimensional
sex machines who have
bum fun at any given
opportunity, day or night.
This isn't true
(for most of us!).

There isn't just one way for two men to have sex, any more than there's just one way for straight people to have sex, and some gay couples never have anal sex at all. But the odds are, if you're a young gay or bi dude, you're probably curious about how it all works. Here's a guide to having safe, enjoyable, connected and fulfilling anal sex.

Is it even your thing?

The best way to figure out if you enjoy action around the anus is to honestly listen to your body and its urges. Many young guys are turned on by the idea of it and seek out ways to experiment. This is probably a sign that you're a bottom – you might like to receive anal sex.

For someone like me on the other hand, being a bottom just isn't right. When I was younger, I wanted to know what all the fuss was about with anal sex, so I played with myself using fingers and subsequently allowed two guys to put their penises in me. I HATED IT.

It felt uncomfortable, painful and like the most unsexy thing in the world. Pain is your body's way of telling you something ain't right, so listen to it!

Maybe you love the idea of penetrating someone else, but you don't like the idea of being penetrated yourself. That might mean you're a top – someone who likes to give anal sex.

Loads of guys are versatile (or "verse") – they like to give and receive, chopping and changing depending on their mood and who their partner is.

Maybe you don't feel like you're a top, a bottom OR a verse. Maybe you're something else: a side. Clinical sexologist Dr. Joe Kort describes it well:

"Sides prefer to kiss, hug and engage in oral sex, rimming, mutual masturbation and rubbing up and down on each other, to name just a few of the sexual activities they enjoy. These men enjoy practically every sexual practice aside from anal penetration of any kind. They may have tried it, and even performed it for some time, before they became aware that for them, it was simply not erotic and wasn't getting any more so."

Even for the most practised bottom, there might be some degree of mild pain at the beginning of a sexual encounter. This is a signal to slow down. It could also mean that tonight just isn't your night. And that is okay. It's your body and your health so the top you're with will have to wait. On the plus side, there are SO many other things you can do. The moral of the story is, trust your gut (in more ways than one).

Practise makes perfect

Before you ever let a dude put his ding dong anywhere near your bum, you should get used to the feeling of having something in and around that area. Playing with yourself down there will help you understand how elastic your back passage is and will make the feeling less weird and frightening.

If you want to try this, start slowly, ideally using a water-based lube, perhaps with your baby finger. Take it easy and make sure you have flat short nails as you don't want a nasty cut inside your rectum. Then try masturbating at the same time.

If you begin to feel more confident over time, then perhaps try two fingers. Never experiment with household objects which are not designed for anal play. They could cut you, leave harmful paint or a chemical residue behind or you may unintentionally suck an object up your bum and not be able to get it out.

If you're in trouble, then seek medical help right away. Believe me, they've probably seen far worse than a carrot stuck up a young guy's bum!

Be mentally connected

It may come as a shock, but there is a very real connection between your head and your bum. Ask anyone who has had anal sex and they will tell you that a smooth and enjoyable ride can become uncomfortable and painful when you're not mentally prepared. You quite literally close up!

Your rectum is surrounded by a thick wall of muscle and then there are two contracting holes – yes, you heard me correctly, TWO! The first one is on the outside of the body and the second is about 15 centimetres inside you. It's there to regulate the movement of gas and solid waste (sorry). Studies have shown that external influences like how you're feeling and where you are can cause one or both of the anal openings to loosen or tighten.

Breathe deeply, don't rush things and consciously try to loosen the muscles of your body. And if you want to feel really comfortable, you need to be with someone you trust.

Find someone you trust

You're quite literally letting someone inside you – make sure it's a person you know and trust before they thrust!

I asked some of my friends who enjoy bottoming about the importance of being with a top who cares. They all said it's vital. A person who treats you like a rag doll to be thrown about isn't the person you should be experimenting with.

A person who treats you like a rag doll to be thrown about isn't the person you should be experimenting with.

Before you get down to business, have an open and honest chat about what you want from the experience. Ask your partner about their desires, tell them it's your first time and that they need to be patient, and that they'll need to follow **your** lead. Just because you're a bottom, that doesn't mean you can't be in command. It's known as being a bossy bottom or a power bottom – we love a good label, don't we?

In the heat of the moment you may just decide to go for it and pretend you're more experienced than you are. This could end up being very painful and potentially dangerous. No matter how ready you think you are, always have the chat.

Getting clean

You can't have bum sex without thinking about poos. It's always best to keep poo and sex separate, so it's a good idea to think about how to keep clean before jumping into bed.

Getting clean doesn't need to involve scary hose pipes and industrial water jets. The most important thing to consider is diet and timing.

First things first: try to do a poo before you have sex. To keep your bowel movements regular and – just as important – solid, each high-fibre foods like brown rice, brown bread, nuts, broccoli and fibre-rich cereals. It goes without saying that eating spicy foods before anal sex is a bad idea.

Next, clean your bum. Some people clean inside their rectum with water. This is called douching. Lots of people don't douche, though – it takes some pre-planning, and some people think it might be harmful, because you could end up damaging the bum's mucus lining, which stops your bum tearing and therefore helps protect you from STIs. It might be enough to just use a finger. Inspect and clean the area by sliding your finger in and out while you're in the shower. This will double up as a loosening exercise before you hop into bed with whoever your lucky partner is, too.

Use the right lubricant and protection

The inside of your anus is a delicate place. It has a thin lining which can easily damaged, which means anal sex is an easy way to catch a whole host of nasty STIs. Because of this, it's important to always wear a correctly sized condom and to use a thick water-based lube. Oil-based lube (and things like Vaseline and baby oil) will make the condom weak and more likely to break. It's a good idea to carry a condom or two and a little sachet of lube in your wallet when you're out and about so you're never without protection!

There may be a mess. So what?!

There's no way of being 100% certain that you'll make no mess when you're having anal sex. After all, someone is penetrating your poop shoot. You may also find that you're extremely gassy in the hours following sex – that's just the air that's been pushed inside you leaving your body bit by bit.

If there's a mess, stay calm, clean up and try to see the funny side with your partner. If you're a top and this happens, BE NICE to your partner and reassure them that everything is fine. If they feel judged or ashamed, it will certainly affect your bond and any future sexual encounters you may have.

Having anal sex is a learning process. The more you learn about you body, and the more you practice, the fewer mishaps you'll have. Be kind to yourself and know that it's all part of the process.

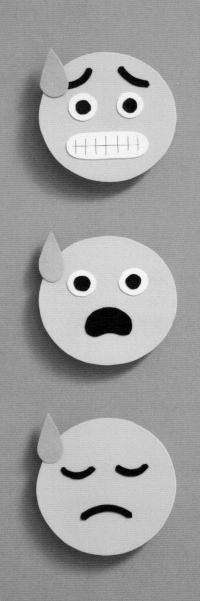

36

DELAYED & PREMATURE EJACULATION

If there's one thing that will wreck your sex buzz, it's performance anxiety. It's easy for people with a penis to worry about how long they'll be able to keep an erection, or how long it takes them to cum.

Lots of things can change how long it takes us to reach the point of orgasm and some of them will be out of your control. So first of all, cut yourself a little slack. The body and mind work incredibly closely when you're aroused and sometimes things will happen in a way you didn't expect or want them to. It happens to everyone.

The body and mind work incredibly closely when you're aroused and sometimes things will happen in a way you didn't expect or want them to.

Premature ejaculation

So you're with someone and they start touching you, and before you even really get going, your one-eyed trouser snake decides to spray his venom. Uh oh. What now? The good thing is, this means that your pipes are working, and they're responding to what you're seeing or feeling. Cumming too early can make you feel a bit bad about yourself. Porn and even mainstream film and TV shows make it look as though a "real" man can go at vigorously it for hours and hours without out cumming. This is not true. If it was, the world's population would be greatly reduced – most guys can't thrust for more than ten minutes without passing out from exhaustion! Britain's National Health Service did a study on how long sex lasts. They looked at 500 couples from five countries, and found that the average time taken to ejaculate during intercourse was around 5.5 minutes. Every guy has premature ejaculation every so often. But if it happens to them more than half the time they have sex, they should get checked out by a doctor just in case.

> **Porn and even mainstream film and TV shows make it look as though a "real" man can go at vigorously it for hours and hours without cumming. This is not true.**

Possible causes

- Stress – someone might experience premature ejaculation if they're worried about other things going on in their life
- Anxiety about sex
- Taking drink and drugs
- They might have conditioned themselves, through masturbation, to come quickly.
- Biological reasons – some people have extra-sensitive penises.

Things that can help

- Masturbating a couple of hours before sex to lessen the libido a little
- Using extra-thick condoms to reduce the sensitivity of the penis
- Stopping and taking a deep breath
- Trying other positions that are less stimulating
- Taking little breaks during sex, or thinking about something boring!

Delayed ejaculation

When someone's suffering from delayed ejaculation, their partner might be thrilled at first – the sex lasts for ages! But in time, it can be frustrating. If your partner doesn't ejaculate, it can make you feel like you're not sexy enough to make them climax. If you suffer from it, it can make you feel broken in some way. But you're not!

Possible causes

- Over-exposure to porn
- Masturbating in a way that can't be replicated through sex with someone else
- Circumcision, which leaves the penis desensitized
- Diabetes
- Surgery to the bladder or prostate gland
- Spinal cord injury
- Drink and drugs
- Stress and anxiety

Things that can help

- Avoiding porn
- Masturbating less often
- Trying a different masturbation technique
- Counselling
- Drinking less alcohol
- Using sex toys that stimulate the penis
- Playing slow sex games
- Using stimulating creams or lubes

If all else fails and there is no improvement, then as always, go and see your GP. They won't shame or embarrass you but could refer you to an expert.

My biggest piece of advice is to find a partner who is patient and understanding. I've been in situations where guys got angry and asked, "What's wrong, why can't you cum?" and I can tell you, it doesn't feel nice. If anything, it makes the problem worse.

If your partner gets frustrated with you, then tell them how it's making you feel. If they don't change their tone, move on and find someone who enjoys the gift of having sex with you whether you cum in seconds or don't cum at all.

Li from Beijing said:

"My partner was very understanding when I had trouble trying to finish off during sex. He would try everything he could to arouse me but this would usually make me feel more worried and unable to get there.

I eventually realized that I was thinking of unrelated things when I was having sex: work, money, time, what I was going to make for dinner. I had to shut that out and be 100% in the moment. I also tried laying off the porn and masturbation for three weeks, which really helped. I started to feel more and more attracted to my partner again.

I still take longer than him to cum and sometimes I don't cum at all, but we both understand each other's bodies and don't put pressure on it. If it happens it happens. If it doesn't then that's fine."

Shane Jenek

Shane is an activist, singer, TV host and drag artist (performing under the name Courtney Act). Courtney was a finalist on *RuPaul's Drag Race* Season Six – and the winner of *Celebrity Big Brother* UK.

Dear 16-year-old Shane: relax! I know you are worried: worried about being rejected for who you are, worried whether there is a place for a person like you in the world... you worry so much, and I don't blame you. People will tell you that who you are is wrong. People will tell you to stop doing what you love because it's wrong (don't worry, you won't listen to them). Work hard, focus on what makes you happy and what excites you, and have as much fun as possible. You are feminine and you are masculine and that is OK. You are allowed to be a feminine boy. Life is long and the race is only with yourself – there will be good bits and bad bits and they are all important and valuable. You will deny and push against your sexuality and gender trying to fit in, thinking they are a weakness, but the plot twist is that when you release the shame and lean into the fear something magical will happen: those things you thought were your weaknesses will become your greatest strengths. And also, please please please love your body the way it is. It's beautiful. The images of gay mens' bodies you will see in pop culture will make you feel like your body isn't good enough. It is. Enjoy it and let other people enjoy it too. Also appreciate your full, youthful hairline cause that won't be with you forever.

37

CUMMING!

Here's a nugget of information that I've never shared with anyone beyond my best friend and mother (yes, we talk about this kind of stuff)! Until I was 27, I could only cum by stimulating myself – I had never cum from someone else touching me, or from having penetrative sex.

I think that's partly because of the psychological and physical effects of my circumcision, but also because I suffered from sexual shame and performance anxiety, and because I had never felt connected enough to my previous partners to fully let go. The moment it happened for the first time, I felt like crying and screaming from the rooftops "PRAISE RUPAUL, I JIZZED IN HIM, I JIZZED IN HIM, I JIZZED IN HIM!" I didn't, you'll be glad to hear.

The moment it happened for the first time, I felt like crying and screaming from the rooftops.

There are many factors that determine how easy or difficult it can be to cum in different situations:

- Nerves
- Stress
- How much porn you've been watching
- Hormone levels

- Your level of attraction to your sexual partner
- Lack of body confidence
- Mood

- The last time you ejaculated
- Feeling pressure from a sexual partner (or from yourself)

All, some or none of these factors can be at play while you're in the middle of getting down and dirty with yourself or someone else, and sometimes they can get in the way of the fun.

Everyone's body and sexual journey is different. When I relieved myself of the pressure to be, act and perform a certain way in the bedroom, I became a more authentic and loving partner – and more loving towards myself, too. You can do the same. Cut the pressure, add the fun.

Everyone's body and sexual journey is different.

Jordan from Galway says:

"I found my first boyfriend on an app. Not the dirty one. The other one. Our relationship started as a one-night stand in the back of his Volkswagen Golf while we were parked up in a closed industrial estate. Sexy. I didn't tell him, but it was the first time I had ever done anything beyond kissing and over-trouser touching with another guy. I was so excited, my heart was pounding as he slowly kissed his way from my neck down to my crotch. This was it. My first hand or blowjob was about to happen! But as he started to stroke my penis, I began to feel confused, then angry, then worried. Why was I not feeling all the explosive sensations I saw people experiencing in movie sex scenes? I took my manhood back from him, and quickly realized it was the grip, pressure and position of his hand that weren't working for me. Once I had taken back command, it all felt great again. I felt bad for him but I didn't want to waste his time or energy so I finished myself off."

Jordan was experiencing something that almost every guy will go through. The inability to reach climax through stimulation from another person or from simple penetrative or oral sex. This is nothing to be worried about and WAY WAY WAY more common than you may think. There's nothing wrong with masturbating during sex. If you're having sex with someone and they want to touch themselves rather than having you touch them, this doesn't mean you're bad in bed!

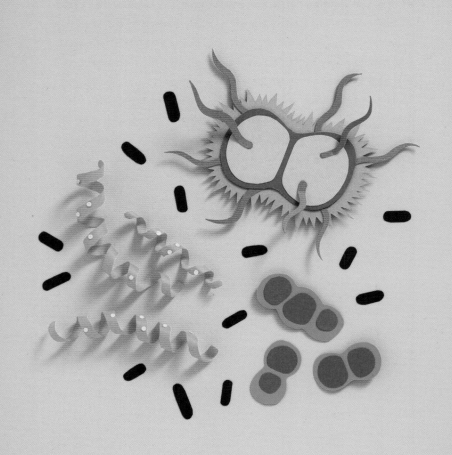

38

SEXUALLY TRANSMITTED INFECTIONS

"If you have sex you will get an infection and die!"

This was the kind of fearmongering I used to get from my early sex-ed teachers. As you can imagine, hearing that you'd probably die if you had sex was terrifying for young Riyadh, who was randy as hell and dying to start bonking.

You'll be happy to hear that in reality it's not quite as doom and gloom as that.

Sex is a gift. It's glorious, free and thrilling, and you can experience it over and over again throughout your life. Sex can bring you closer to yourself and to other people. But the more sexual partners you have, the more likely you are to get sexually transmitted infections

Sex is a gift – but the more sexual partners you have, the more likely you are to get sexually transmitted infections.

(also known as STIs). STIs can be serious, and statistically speaking, gay men are more at risk than other people. There is only one way to fix that: STOP HAVING SEX. Only joking!

If you're ready to go all the way – if you're over the age of consent, and with someone you trust – make sure you have **safe** sex. But what does "safe sex" actually mean? Safe sex is all about being aware of the risks you're taking, learning how to use condoms and then actually USING THEM. Safe sex also means having regular check ups at a sexual health clinic, even if you're using protection.

How do STIs spread?

STIs are most commonly passed from one person to another through penetrative sex and the exchange of bodily fluids like semen, blood, and vaginal and anal fluid. But certain infections can also be passed through kissing or touch. For example, genital herpes can be passed on by mere skin-on-skin contact.

You can never tell if someone has an STI or not simply by looking at them. Saying that, it's always a good idea to be conscious of sores, rashes or discharge around the genital area of someone you're about to have sex with. It's okay to say no if you notice something that makes you unsure.

Here are some of the most common STIs, how they are transmitted, the symptoms they show and the treatment available.

Chlamydia

Symptoms

- Pain when urinating

- White, cloudy or watery discharge from the tip of the penis

- Burning or itching in the urethra (the tube that carries urine out of the body)

- Pain in the testicles

- But you might not have any symptoms – that's why it's important to get checked regularly.

How is it passed on?
Passed on primarily during anal or vaginal sex. It is less likely to be transmitted through oral sex

How is it treated?
Antibiotics (a doctor will prescribe you these)

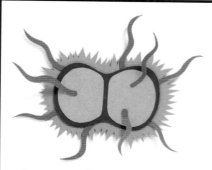

Gonorrhea

Symptoms

- An unusual discharge from the tip of the penis, which may be white, yellow or green

- Pain or a burning sensation when urinating

- Inflammation (swelling) of the foreskin

- Pain or tenderness in the testicles – this is rare

- In people who get periods, bleeding between periods.

How is it passed on?

- Unprotected sex, including oral sex

- Sharing sex toys that haven't been washed or covered with a new condom each time

How is it treated?
Antibiotics

Syphilis

Symptoms
- The main symptom is a small, painless sore or ulcer called a chancre that you might not notice
- The sore will typically be on the penis, vagina, or around the anus, although they can sometimes appear in the mouth or on the lips, fingers or buttocks
- Most people only have one sore, but some people have several
- Swollen glands in your neck, groin or armpits.

How is it passed on?
Close contact with an infected syphilis sore. This usually happens during vaginal, anal or oral sex, or by sharing sex toys with someone who's infected

How is it treated?
Antibiotics

Crabs

Symptoms
- Irritating itch
- Inflammation from scratching
- Black powder in your underwear
- Blue spots or small spots of blood on your skin (caused by lice bites), often on your thighs or lower abdomen.

How is it passed on?
- Close bodily contact with an infected person

How is it treated?
Can be treated at home with insecticide cream, lotion or shampoo

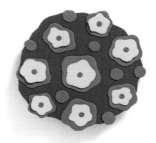

Human Papillomavirus (HPV)

Symptoms

- Some forms of HPV have been known to cause cancer in men and women if left untreated.

- It can cause genital warts which can become uncomfortable, itchy, inflamed or bleeding

How is it passed on?

- It's highly contagious and spreads during sexual intercourse and skin-to-skin contact of the genital areas.

How is it treated?

There is a vaccine to prevent HPV, but no cure

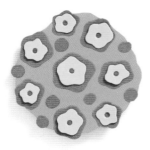

Herpes

Symptoms

- Small blisters that burst to leave red, open sores around your genitals, anus, thighs or buttocks

- Tingling, burning or itching around your genitals

- Pain when you pee

- In people with vaginas, discharge that's not usual for you

How is it passed on?

- Skin-to-skin contact with the infected area

- Unprotected sex, including oral sex

- By sharing sex toys with someone who has herpes

How is it treated?

There's no cure but the blisters usually go away on their own in time. The symptoms can be improved with antiviral medication.

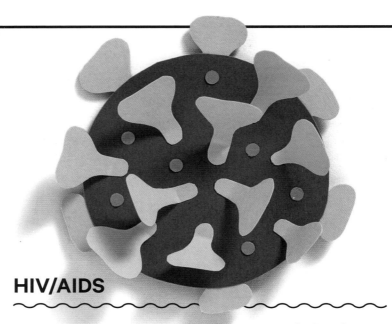

HIV/AIDS

In 1981, 121 previously healthy young gay men died in the USA of a mysterious new illness. Scientists started to call it Acquired Immune Deficiency Syndrome (AIDS). AIDS is actually a collection of different illnesses that you can pick up if you've been infected with the Human Immunodeficiency Virus (HIV). At first, HIV/ AIDS was seen as a "gay" disease, since so many gay men were affected, and it led to a huge rise in homophobia. Actually HIV can be passed on through heterosexual sex too – it's transmitted when bodily fluids like semen and blood are shared, so it can be passed on by sharing needles or through blood transfusions

If you're having sex, ALWAYS use protection and GET TESTED REGULARLY!

as well as through sex. But the majority of people who are diagnosed with HIV in the UK and USA are still men who have sex with men.

In the 1980s and 1990s, almost everyone who was diagnosed with HIV developed AIDS and the mortality rate was extremely high – there is no cure, and at first there was no effective treatment. But the GOOD news is there are really effective treatments now, and people who are diagnosed early and get treated can live as long as people who don't have HIV. There's even evidence that people responding well to treatment can't pass the HIV virus to others. The BAD news is that 12% of people living with HIV in the UK don't even know they have it, and they aren't being treated. So if you're having sex, ALWAYS use protection and GET TESTED REGULARLY!

Symptoms

- A short, flu-like illness shortly after you are infected with HIV

- After that, many people don't have any symptoms for years.

How is it passed on?

- Having heterosexual or homosexual sex without a condom

- Sharing sex toys

- Sharing drug injecting equipment

- Mothers can pass it to children in the womb, or while breastfeeding

- Coming into contact with contaminated blood

- You CAN'T catch HIV by kissing, hugging, shaking hands, sharing a toilet or sharing plates, cutlery or cups.

How is it treated?

Emergency drugs called PEP can prevent people becoming infected if used up to 72 hours after infection. If someone tests as HIV positive, anti-retroviral drugs are used to stop the virus replicating in the body.

Three cheers for condoms

A rubber, Johnny, love glove – whatever you call it, the condom is the best way of protecting yourself from STIs and stopping them spreading. But even though condoms are great, they don't work 100% of the time. They can split, slide off or not capture semen correctly. Here are a few ways to make your condom use as protective as possible:

- Always use a condom that fits. Too tight and it may burst, too loose and it may slide off mid-action

- Use plenty of water-based lube. Lubricants containing oil can degrade the latex in the condom making it weak and more likely to split

- Never put lube on your penis (or someone else's) **before** the condom goes on. This makes it more likely that the condom will slide off

- Avoid thin condoms – they're more likely to tear

- Like with a pot of jam, always make sure the condom is within its use-by date

- If you're allergic to latex, get latex-free condoms from a pharmacy or sexual health clinic

- Never use teeth or a sharp object to open a condom wrapper. Once you've opened the wrapper, examine the rubber for tears.

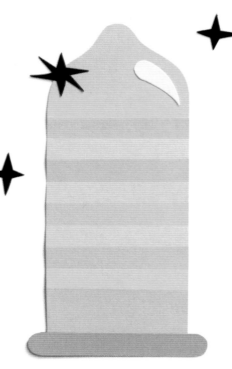

What if I get an STI?

Don't panic! Most STIs are treatable with the right medication. If you have symptoms, don't have sex without a condom until you've finished your treatment. Go to a sexual health clinic for a check up.

Doctors and nurses at sexual health clinics won't judge you – they've seen and heard it all before. The great thing about going to an STI clinic is you'll get an appointment sooner than you would at your regular doctor, you don't have to give your real name, and you'll get your results quickly.

Doctors and nurses at sexual health clinics won't judge you – they've seen and heard it all before.

If you're ever worried or confused about any of this stuff (there's A LOT to take in!) then speak to your doctor or staff at a sexual health clinic who will be able to give you the information you need.

Have safe fun guys!

 If you live in a city there's probably a sexual health clinic near you where you can access free STI screening, condoms and lubricant.

Dr Ranj Singh

Dr Ranj Singh is a doctor specializing in children's health, as well as a writer and presenter. Alongside his work as an NHS doctor, he presented the CBeebies show *Get Well Soon*, appears as the resident doctor on *This Morning* and writes columns for *Attitude* magazine and Netdoctor.

No one is expecting you to be perfect. Just be the best version of yourself. These are the words I've learned to tell myself time and time again. Sometimes it can feel like everyone around you is expecting you to be a certain way because they think that's what will make you happy. They don't mean any harm – they just want what's best for you. It's important to hear them, but at the end of the day, you know and create your own happiness. Let yourself be the amazing person you are inside. Let your voice be heard. Reach for your star, grab it and show the world what you can do. Be yourself and be the very best you can be. Because in my eyes, you are perfect.

39

MY FIRST TIME

Well, it wouldn't be a book about sexuality if I didn't share the tale of my first time, would it? If you've skipped the rest of the book and come straight here... congratulations. You are thirsty as hell.

I'm one of the lucky ones. When I think back to my first time, it brings a warm smile to my face – unlike many of my friends, who wince and cringe at memories of fumbling around the back of a grimy Renault Clio, trying to look sexy while almost impaling themselves on the gearstick! No, my first time had all the ingredients of a perfect first encounter with another guy. It was scary, exciting, forbidden, erotic, exhilarating and breathtaking. I'm smiling and my heart is beating a little faster as I write this, just thinking about it.

I now realize that I've never given my handsome deflowerer a name or described what he looked like. Let's call him Andy. He was taller than me, and he had beautiful piercing eyes and a cute boy-next-door face with a touch of light teen stubble on his chin (it had taken him two years to grow it). His skin was like porcelain velvet to the touch and his body had this natural "I didn't even try" rippling toned feel. I think you get the idea. I thought I had won the man lottery.

So back in the First Kiss chapter, I left you with an image of us pressed up against a Nissan Micra. The only light came from dim, yellowish street lamps, so we felt somewhat protected, like no one would see us. We began touching each other and as we started having oral sex I heard the clip-clop of high heels coming down the road towards us. NOOOO!

We quickly started buttoning ourselves up and stood far apart, pretending to bitch about one of the girls from school. I said, "Ugh, Carla is so annoying the way she does that thing, right?!" The group of two girls and two guys briefly looked at us as they walked by. We were safe. They had no idea what we were up to.

What makes this story even more intense is that although I was so out of the closet, my name should have been GAY-briel, Andy was not. He was terrified of anyone finding out his secret. I didn't really mind if anyone knew what I was doing, but of course I had to respect his desire to keep this midnight rendezvous absolutely private... ;)

Once the people had passed by, and their chatter had slowly faded into the night, I made an executive decision: we needed to change tactics so we could continue our fab night of fornication in peace.

I grabbed Andy's hand and we ran down the road to a small, dark forested area. (I promise this isn't about to turn into a cheap murder mystery.) Our eyes took a while to adjust to the darkness, and we slowly pushed our way through the branches, tripping over logs and a trench, until we came across a clearing. The floor was flat and covered in leaves.

Andy didn't really say anything, but he didn't need to. His deep breathing, passionate kisses and the way he held onto my hand were enough.

We lay down on the wet leaves with our bare white bums out. This was around November, so it was freezing, but that didn't stop us. Before I knew it, we were entangled in each other's bodies. The cold of the forest made the warmth of his body even more incredible.

We got down to business, which didn't last very long, but one thing has always stood out and makes me laugh every time I think about it. As we were in the throes of passion, he involuntarily called out the name of the uber-hot jock in our year that everyone fancied: "Ugh, Sam, mmmm." I stopped for a second and just looked at him as if to say, "Are you serious?!" before realizing that I ABSOLUTELY agreed with him. So I said, "Yeah, Sam is so hot, isn't he?" and we carried on.

It all seemed to finish as quickly as it had begun. Andy said he needed to get back to the house party or people would start to wonder what was going on. I agreed and we got dressed.

We didn't have anal sex that night, but I still count this as the moment I lost my virginity. As I said in the Let's Talk About Sex chapter, sex can come in many forms and it isn't always about a penis penetrating a bum or a vagina. This was the most erotic experience of my life and the most intimate I had ever been with another person. So, for me, and I presume him, it was absolutely VIRGINITY-SMASHING SEX!

We walked out of the forest and back onto the path, where we saw ourselves under street lamps for the first time, and it was a sight. Andy's left side was covered with wet brown mud, and he had leaves and twigs in his hair. But I was immaculate. Not even a bit of dust. It was a modern gay miracle.

Like a pair of undercover secret agents, we decided to split up and re-enter the party from different directions, five minutes apart. We also came up with a story to explain why Andy was so destroyed by mud: "I slipped into a puddle." Believable.

We both got back to the party didn't speak again that night, but I was buzzing. I felt like after all these years, I had finally arrived (and so had my burning sexuality). There was no stopping me now!

THAT'S IT!

If there's one thing I'd like you to take from reading this book, it's that being gay is a gift and absolutely worth living for. That goes for the entire spectrum of other queer identities, too.

At times you will be treated differently because of your sexuality, you will need to defend yourself, you will likely suffer heartbreak, you will be confused about your feelings and some people just won't get you. This doesn't mean you aren't worthy of the same happiness and chance of a fulfilling life as other people are. Other people's issues are exactly that: theirs, not yours.

The world is ready for your light and individuality. When you're ready, and only on your own terms, let it shine free.

Because you're an LGBT+ person, you have the rare ability to understand what it means to be a minority, to be different, to be special. You will see the world around you through a different lens than other people and you'll find it easier to have empathy and understanding for people who aren't like you. Use this superpower to do something amazing with your life. Help those who need it, both in your community and outside of it.

When you feel angry at the world or defeated by homophobic discrimination, just think back to the progress made by members of our LGBT+ family who came before you. Change is slow, but it is inevitable. The one thing that can hurry it up is being visible, and using your voice to demand equality and positive representation. The world is ready for your light and individuality. When you're ready, and only on your own terms, let it shine free. We need more people like you to move this story to the next chapter.

Remember that a new generation will come along after you to take up the queer baton and run forward with it. Welcome them with open arms and become the role model you needed when you were growing up.

Finally, remember what this journey is all about in the first place: love. Make the journey worth it. Love unapologetically, love without fear, and love hard.

USEFUL CONTACTS

In this section you'll find some organizations and websites where you can find help and advice for all sorts of issues. Many of these organizations offer international support over the phone or by email.

United Kingdom

EMERGENCY SERVICES: 999/112

Childline
0800 1111
www.childline.org.uk

A free counselling service for children and young people up to the age of 19

LGBT Foundation
0345 3 30 30 30
The LGBT foundation offers advice and support to LGBT people.

LGBT Helpline Scotland
0300 123 2523

Samaritans
116 123
A free, 24-hour confidential helpline. You can talk about anything you want, without judgement.

Switchboard
0300 330 0630
Switchboard is an LGBT+ helpline. They're at the end of the phone, and will help you about absolutely anything you want to talk about, without judgment.

Albert Kennedy Trust
www.akt.org.uk
The Albert Kennedy Trust supports young LGBT+ people who are experiencing homelessness or living in hostile situations to find safe homes, education, training and mentoring and to celebrate their identities.

Mermaids UK
mermaidsuk.org.uk

An organization supporting transgender and non-binary young people and their families.

NHS
www.nhs.uk/live-well

The NHS Live Well website has loads of great advice about staying healthy, with specific sections on sexual and mental health for LGBT+ people.

Stonewall
www.stonewall.org.uk
08000 50 20 20
Stonewall is a charity that aims to make life better for all LGBT+ people. They have great resources on their web-site and an information service you can contact for advice.

Terrence Higgins Trust
www.tht.org.uk
The UK's largest HIV and sexual health charity.

Ireland

EMERGENCY SERVICES: 999/112

Samaritans
116 123
A free, 24-hour confidential helpline. You can talk about anything you want, without judgement.

LGBT Ireland Helpline
1890 929 539
A network of trained volunteers who provide a non-judgmental, confidential, listening support and information for LGBT+ people or those questioning their identity

Dublin Lesbian Line
018729911
A helpline for lesbians and others in the LGBT+ community run my volunteers offering confidential, non-judgmental support over the phone. For those outside Dublin too.

Childline
CALL – 180666666
TEXT – 50101
A free and confidential helpline for people under 18. They can offer support for a number of issue like sexuality and relationships, mental health, eating disorders, issues at home and bullying.

BeLongTo
belongto.org

National LGBT+ youth service for people aged between 14 and 23 years with a focus on mental and sexual health, alongside drug and alcohol support.

LGBT Ireland
lgbt.ie

A network of trained volunteers who provide a non-judgemental, confidential, listening support and information for LGBT+ people or those questioning their identity

Amach! LGBT
amachlgbt.com

A full range of services for LGBTQ+ people in the Galway area and surrounding regions. Support areas include: Coming out, trans community issues, youth groups, elderly support and learning for families.

Focus Ireland
www.focusireland.ie

Ireland's leading not for profit working to prevent people becoming, remaining or returning to homelessness.

Gay Men's Health Service / HSE
www.hse.ie/eng/services/list/5/sexhealth/gmhs/

Ireland's only dedicated statutory sexual health and wellbeing service for gay and bisexual men, men who have sex with men and the trans population.

Transgender Equality Network Ireland
www.teni.ie

TENI works with Trans people offering peer support groups, crisis support, information for families and healthcare guidance.

Childline
www.childline.ie

A free and confidential helpline for people under 18. They can offer support for a number of issue like sexuality and relationships, mental health, eating disorders, issues at home and bullying.

Australia

EMERGENCY SERVICES: 000

Q LIFE
1800184527
Anonymous, LGBT+ peer support line and referral for people wanting to talk about a range of issues including sexuality, identity, gender, bodies, feelings or relationships.

Lifeline
131114
24 hour crisis support and suicide prevention helpline for all Australians

Suicide Call Back Service

1300659467

A national 24 hour telehealth provider that offers free professional phone and online counselling for people living in Australia.

Kids Helpline

1800551800

A national helpline for young people (5-25) looking for support with mental health, identity, family issues, sex and relationships and many other concerns.

Parents, Family and Friends of Lesbians and Gays

pflagaustralia.org.au

A service with a mission of keeping families together. They offer learning support and advice for those closest to an LGBT+ person.

ACON

www.acon.org.au

An organization for HIV prevention, HIV support and lesbian, gay, bisexual, transgender and intersex (LGBTI) health in general.

Q switchboard

www.switchboard.org.au

A peer based, volunteer run support service for LGBT+ people, their friends, families and allies.

Mental Health Online

www.mentalhealthonline. org.au

Free of charge online mental health services through self-assessment, self-help and, if you choose, online professional support.

TRANCEND

www.transcendsupport. com.au

Transcend provides support for the parents and carers of young trans people offering community connection, information, advocacy & fundraising.

The Gender Centre

gendercentre.org.au

An accommodation service and also act as an education, support, training and referral resource for people with gender issues.

Kids Under Cover

www.kuc.org.au

An organization dedicated to preventing young people becoming homeless within Australia.

New Zealand

EMERGENCY SERVICES: 111

OUTLine NZ

0800 688 5463

Helpline for all situations. Able to talk about loneliness and isolation, sexuality and gender identity, sexual health, relationships and meeting people, STIs and HIV, legal and ethical issues, and many more.

Samaritans

0800 726 666

A free, 24-hour confidential helpline. You can talk about anything you want, without judgement.

Youth Line

CALL – 0800376633

TEXT – 234

Free nationwide helpline service for young people of all backgrounds and identities. They provide specialist training and development too.

RainbowYOUTH

www.ry.org.nz

Support for LGBT+ people up to the age of 27. They offer education resources, non-judgemental advice, safe meeting spaces, peer support groups and more.

I'm Local Project
www.imlocal.co.nz

National network directory of local LGBT+ support organizations specializing in different areas of work

Auckland Sexual Health Services
www.ashs.org.nz

LGBT+ friendly STI screening and treatment services.

Gender Minorities Aotearoa
genderminorities.com

Transgender led organization. They deliver education and training, run a national database of information and resources, operate The Gender Centre in Wellington and run regular free sober social events.

South Africa

EMERGENCY SERVICES
Ambulance: 10177
Police: 10111

Childline South Africa
0800055555
A free crisis telephone counselling line deals with hundreds of queries from children and adults.

LifeLine
0816322322
24 hour free counselling and information line for people of all backgrounds

AIDS Helpline
0800012322
Offering advice, information and treatment for people affected by HIV/AIDS. Able to answer questions if you think you've been exposed to the virus.

OUT
www.out.org.za

OUT provides health services to LGBT+ people including targeted HIV/AIDS work, counselling, a vibrant community centre, community building programmes and support groups.

LGBT+ Forum
www.lgbtforum.org

An umbrella organization for LGBT+ employees who want to safe workplaces

USA

EMERGENCY SERVICES: 911

The Trevor Project
(866) 488-7386
Helpline providing crisis intervention and suicide prevention services for LGBT+ young people aged 13–24.

The Trans Lifeline
United States
1-877-565-8860
A 24/7 support helpline staffed by transgender people for transgender people.

GLBT National Help Centre
1-888-843-4564
Provides support over the phone, online or via email. They speak with callers of all ages about bullying, workplace issues, STIs, coming out, relationships, safer sex and more.

National Coalition for the Homeless
1-800-621-4000
If you're a teenager and are thinking about running away from home, or if you are already living on the streets, call the National Runaway Switchboard.

For Mom and Dad. Thank you for never doubting my wild dreams, for the unconditional love and being my rock. I love you – Riyadh x

Inspiring | Educating | Creating | Entertaining

Brimming with creative inspiration, how-to projects, and useful information to enrich your everyday life, Quarto Knows is a favourite destination for those pursuing their interests and passions. Visit our site and dig deeper with our books into your area of interest: Quarto Creates, Quarto Cooks, Quarto Homes, Quarto Lives, Quarto Drives, Quarto Explores, Quarto Gifts, or Quarto Kids.

First Published in 2019 by Frances Lincoln Children's Books, an imprint of The Quarto Group. The Old Brewery, 6 Blundell Street, London N7 9BH, United Kingdom
T (0)20 7700 6700 F (0)20 7700 8066 **www.QuartoKnows.com**

ISBN 978-1-78603-191-4

The illustrations were created using cut paper, and digitally.
Set in Sentinel

Published by Rachel Williams
Designed by Melissa McFeeters
Edited by Kate Davies
Production by Jenny Cundill and Kate O'Riordon

Manufactured in Ljubljana, Slovenia DZS 12019

9 8 7 6 5 4 3 2 1

The Switchboard is a toll-free, confidential hotline.

National AIDS Hotline
1-800-232-4636
Call for information about HIV/AIDS, how to prevent transmission, STI screening services and treatment.

▇e Trevor Project
▇.thetrevorproject.org
▇national organization providing crisis intervention and suicide prevention services to LGBT+ young people aged 13–24.

The Human Rights Campaign
www.hrc.org

An LGBT+ equal rights organization. Their website has information about laws and the rights of LGBT+ people across various American States.

LGBTQ+ sexual health
www.cdc.gov/lgbthealth

This site has resources including a geographic guide on where to seek an STI screening, how to have safe sex, where to get access to condoms and what to do if you think you've picked up an STI.

Mental Health America
www.mentalhealthamerica.net/lgbt

A directory of locations across America where you can access face-to-face help for mental health issues. They have LGBT+-specific support pages and self-screening questionnaires for depression, anxiety and other issues.

National Coalition for the Homeless
nationalhomeless.org/issues/lgbt/

A multi-organization resource centre for those who are homeless or considering running away from home. They are LGBT+-friendly and offer nationwide support.

National Centre For Transgender Equality
transequality.org

An organization offering medical guidance, support for the family and friends of trans people, education services, homelessness and housing support and more.

Canada

EMERGENCY SERVICES: 911

Youthline
Call: 1-800-268-9688
Text: 647 694 4275
www.youthline.ca

Non-judgemental supportline for all queer, trans and two-spirit people aged 29 and under.

The Trans Lifeline
Canada
1-877-330-6366
A 24/7 support helpline staffed by transgender people for transgender people.

PFLAG
pflagcanada.ca

A national organization offering support around sexual orientation, gender identity and gender expression.

Egale
egale.ca

An organization working to improve the lives of LGBT+ people in Canada.

Qmunity
qmunity.ca

An organization based in Vancouver providing support, training, counselling and social groups for all LGBT+ people.